To Alistair

Ch

Ci

Love F

Lu x

GW01417510

Bloomington Daze

More Town and Gown in Middle America

by

Blaise Cronin

authorHOUSE®

AuthorHouse™
1663 Liberty Drive, Suite 200
Bloomington, IN 47403
www.authorhouse.com
Phone: 1-800-839-8640

First published by AuthorHouse 8/20/2007

ISBN: 978-1-4343-0812-2 (sc)

Library of Congress Control Number: 2007903672

Printed in the United States of America
Bloomington, Indiana

This book is printed on acid-free paper.

For Yvonne, where East meets West

Acknowledgment

Amanda Ciccarelli and Yvonne Rogers were kind enough to read an early draft of *Daze*. My *ridiculus mus* is less illiterate and marginally less indiscrete than would otherwise have been the case. I thank them both while accepting full responsibility for all bloopers of the Handel-instead-of-Haydn variety.

Contents

Parturient montes, nascetur ridiculus mus

Horace, *Ars Poetica*

Give Ear to my Words

This book is a homophone, and its author a homiletic old fogey, which, I suppose, is pretty much what you'd expect if you've read *Bloomington Days*. If, however, you haven't, might I suggest you correct this oversight and visit AuthorHouse's webpage *tout de suite* and order a baker's dozen.

AuthorHouse, fortuitously headquartered in Bloomington, is a—if not *the*—market leader in self-publishing, offering countless dabblers, duds and rejects the means to bring forth the next great American novel. For a few hundred dollars would-be Kerouacs and Pynchons, of which there is no local shortage, can have their moment in the sun and their *magnum opus* —one man's magnum is, of course, another's miniature— in their tremulous palms. Auden, who excoriated what Kingsley Amis called 'Creadive Wriding,' must be harrumphing in his grave.

For a few thousand the company will promote your book such that it might actually attract a flicker of critical or commercial attention, but don't bank on it; these days there are almost as many books as eyeballs. As Stephen Page, chief executive of Faber and Faber, put it recently, authors are 'awash in the effluent of abundance.' If getting rich quick is your goal, pyramid selling is a safer bet than self-publishing. Replace 'poetry' with 'self-published books' in Mr. T.S. Eliot's maxim would be my advice: 'With most categories of books you are aiming to make as much money as possible, with poetry you are aiming to lose as little as possible.'

I am as much a reject—the Indiana University Press and one or two others having spurned *Bloomington Days*: 'focus is rather too local and personal,' opined the Press—as a thick-skinned dud, but at least I am continuing a family tradition by trotting down the vanity publishing path. My four great-aunts, Agnes, Anastasia, Ethel and Lucy, were spinsters all. Lucy chose the cloistered life, joining the Sisters of Mercy. In a sense, I have followed in her footsteps: IU is my monastery only here the wimpled nuns are dons, not that you'll hear that superannuated term used much in this institution.

Anastasia and Agnes both lived to a ripe old age, rattling around in the gloom of *North Lodge*, girlishly regaling us with stories of yesteryear's glitter: Anastasia was adamant that she had sung for the Tsar, though the actual circumstances remain unclear to this day; Agnes prudently asserted no such claim to fame and throughout her life played second fiddle to Stasia the soprano. They might just have found fulfillment of sorts in our somnolent yet beguiling university town. If Santa Barbara was paradise for Baudrillard, might not Bloomington have been A & A's third Heaven?

Which leaves Ethel, who self-published a number of courtly romances. I'd occasionally thumb through these hard-backed harbingers of Harlequin, but they left me, a callow lad, cold: I didn't appreciate our very own 'madwoman in the attic.' Now, of course, it is too late; great-aunt Ethel's literary legacy was sold off with the contents of *North Lodge* (Lot 37: A trunk of Edwardian novels, almanacs and richly illustrated equestrian books), and her mannered prose is forever lost. How long, I wonder, before my maunderings about Townies and Gownies in Middle America are themselves de-accessioned, remaindered, pulped and irrevocably and ignominiously erased from the digital archive? How long before I am consigned, along with Ethel and countless other unrequited authors, to terminal oblivion?

For now, though, it's welcome back to Bloomington—one of 24 so-named towns or cities in the U.S. according to the *Herald-Times* (*H-T*); how far off the mark I was in *Bloomington Days*—and welcome back, too, to Old IU, where dogged aspiration and fragile self-belief help keep third-degree *Weltschmerz* at bay. As readers of *Days* may recall, I hail from Ireland. I don't usually mention Bloomington and my motherland in the same breath, but perhaps there are useful connections to be made. John Updike wrote somewhere of Connemara's 'Becketty nothingness.' I know full well what he meant, even though south central Indiana is as close to Connemara as Purcell is to Shostakovich. Mr. Updike's characterization is not without resonance. The enigmatic Samuel Beckett (who pops up later in these pages) would have had a field day here, for angst is as almost common as seasonal allergies in Bloomington. But he of the 'handsome creviced face' and Giacomettian frame chose Paris and Bloomington chose me. Thus did our scribal lives fork.

So here, in the words of Krapp, I remain 'drowned in dreams and burning to be gone'—but not, rest assured, before a few more svelte vignettes are committed to paper; not before another *amuse-gueule* is served up in advance of the main course that one knows deep, deep down will never see the light of day.

Puff Pellets

'You'll claw yourself with an impish humor that would charm the balls off a pawnbroker's sign.' So writes Frank McCourt of Helen Gurley Brown's *Sex and the Single Girl*. McCourt is no slouch when it comes to doling out pre-partum praise; in the five years following publication of his bestseller, *Angela's Ashes*, he provided jacket puff for at least fifteen books. What Limerick's celebrated son doesn't mention, but *Slate* magazine does, is that Mrs. Brown's husband produced the film version of *Angela's Ashes*. You scratch mine; I'll scratch yours.

Nothing new here. The practice of reciprocal blurbing, otherwise known as 'logrolling,' was exposed entertainingly in the pages of *Spy Magazine* during the nineteen eighties and nineties. The magazine regularly showcased authors who traded sycophantic reviews: 'A triumph of style'— Paul Theroux on Nadine Gordimer's *The Conservationist*; 'His is a large, outrageous talent'— Gordimer on Theroux's *Chicago Loop*.

Blurbs—advance praise, often—are designed to create a buzz and boost sales. The term was coined about 100 years ago by the humorist Gelett Burgess. In *Burgess Unabridged: A New Dictionary of Words You*

Have Always Needed he defined it as a 'flamboyant advertisement…an inspired testimonial.' Today puffery and commercial publishing are inseparable bedfellows, whether we are talking about fiction or non-fiction, trade or academic markets. Indeed, a new lexicon has evolved to capture this publishing epiphenomenon: there are 'blurbers' (a.k.a. 'blurbists,' or in special cases, 'blurb-meisters') who 'blurb' for 'blurbees.' A blurber may be said to 'lend his blurb,' which then appears in 'blurb space.' Pre-publication blurbs are not to be confused with other forms of jacket copy, such as snippets from post-publication reviews. Critical acclaim is one thing, celebrity endorsement another.

Simply put, one author's—for it is often, though not always, a mutuality of authors—reputation is used to launch or buttress another's. Sometimes the authors are peers; sometimes the relationship is asymmetrical, as when a master allows a novice to draw on his reputational stock. Little is to be gained by having a non-entity laud an Alexander Solzhenitsyn, Tom Clancy or J.K. Rowling. However, those of us with book sales mired in the hundreds would hardly demur were a luminary to offer us a blurb. Like it or not, product pumping is commonplace in all corners of the Republic of Letters.

The writing of blurbs can be a serious and time-consuming business. Some authors dutifully read and legitimately praise the works for which they supply blurbs; others are not above granting endorsements for books they have not read—a case of being damned by feigned praise? Some scribblers view blurbing as a drain on their own creative energies, moreover one for which they receive no remuneration. On the other hand, for successful writers there is an element of *noblesse oblige* in crafting blurbs.

The lightweight subject of blurbs has attracted the attention of the heavyweight *Wall Street Journal*, which noted that with 150,000 new book titles being produced annually it is hardly surprising that 'a juicy blurb is considered essential for a fledgling author.' A puff from Toni Morrison or Germaine Greer may well help an aspiring author stand out from the crowd, but if a serial blurber is too liberal with her encomia, Gresham's Law kicks in: a surfeit of gushing blurbs—'tarnished superlatives,' as Christopher Isherwood once described them—may cause potential readers to dismiss genuine praise along with shallow puffery.

Camille Paglia used the pages of *Publishers Weekly* to decry 'a corrupt practice' driven by 'shameless cronyism and grotesque hyperbole.' She has a clause in her own book contracts forbidding the use of blurbs; excerpts from book reviews *are* permissible. Perhaps blurbers should be required to disclose relationships (with fellow authors, editors, agents, publishers) which might constitute a material conflict of interest. Yet, occasions surely exist when there is no commercial conflict of interest between the blurber and blurbee, just as there are occasions when the blurbee is unknown, on either a personal or professional level, to the blurber. Equally, it would be nothing less than remarkable if social ties, loyalties and shared organizational affiliations did not play a part in the dispensing of blurbs, and if cronyism were entirely absent from the system.

The subject of blurbs has attracted a fair amount of attention in both the popular and professional press; humor, indignation, speculation and anecdotage appear in more or less equal measure. One thing is clear; blurbing is *à la mode.* In the fiercely competitive world of bookselling, puffery matters. At least, publishers seem to think it does, which may explain the sheaves of advance praise and critical acclaim that pad out any paperback edition worth its salt. What we don't know is whether and to what extent jacket copy of this kind influences the consumer at point-of-sale. Do publishers puff to good effect or is it all marketing hot air? Do 'back-flap babes' actually increase the consumer's propensity to purchase? I haven't the foggiest idea, but I am reminded of Lord Lever's oft-quoted apothegm: 'I know that half the money I spend on advertising is wasted. The trouble is, I don't know which half.'

But that wasn't going to deter me. I'll take all the shallow puffery I can get. Naïvely, I had sent complimentary copies of *Bloomington Days* to three paragons of Middle America's free press, the *Herald-Times*, *Indiana Daily Student* (*IDS*) and *Bloom* (on which more later), thinking that local interest might ause a jaded sub-editor to take a peek. I was wrong; I received not so much as an acknowledgment, let alone the hoped-for reviews from which I might just have been able to extract one or two words of faint praise. So much, then, for something as pithy and witty as 'Malice in Wonderland' (Jean Cocteau on the waspish Cecil Beaton) appearing on the back cover.

A few foolish friends and colleagues claimed to have read *Bloomington Days* with pleasure and/or amusement—what else could they say when cornered by yours truly, fresh from *Apocalypto* and brandishing cocktail sticks, at a faculty reception? But *if* they meant what they said, then perhaps I could use their kind words to tart up the back cover. As you can see, I am either a bloody good twister of collegial arms or my chosen blurbers have a highly developed sense of *noblesse oblige*, unlike the local hacks. At least I won't have to follow the example of the German composer, Max Reger, who once wrote to a critic: 'I am sitting in the smallest room of my house. I have your review before me. In a moment it will be behind me.'

Dead End

It's hard to miss the black capitals on the sunflower yellow background. The diamond-shaped *memento mori* greets me every time I turn off the High Street into well-tempered Woodstock Place. 'Dead End.' These bluntest of monosyllables are not easily ignored. What's wrong with '*cul-de-sac*,' so beloved of the Old World, at least until meddlesome Prince Charles, not satisfied with labeling a proposed extension to the National Gallery 'a monstrous carbuncle,' denounced the hapless *cul-de-sac* as a cause of crime, car dependence and obesity; or, if we wish to avoid royal ire, while also raising the cultural bar, with *Huis clos*, the title of a Sartre play (sometimes translated as *No Exit*)? Were I a linguist, my fancy might be tickled by 'Glottal Stop.'

And if Hoosiers still can't stomach a *soupçon* of French, well, then, why not the prosaic 'No Outlet'—just as they have a block or two away? It's a bit much having to grapple with existential angst every time I curve the dear old Jag into the home stretch. Not that I was always so well wheeled. My first car was a pistachio-colored Fiat Uno with a

nifty sunroof, features that greatly amused the smart alecks of Scotland's
second city, the undisputed capital of badinage and precipitation.

But back to angst, compound angst. I am by trade an information
scientist and as such all too conscious of my place in the academic jungle.
Remember Lord Rutherford's (was it?) parsimonious classification:
'There are two kinds of science, physics and stamp-collecting.' As
a second-tier stamp-collector I can live with 'No Outlet,' even if it
suggests that there isn't a Ralf Lauren discount store at the end of
the drive—which, though regrettable, is hardly tragic. 'Dead End,'
however, constitutes an irrefragably critical commentary on my life
choices. Okay, so I live in the Midwest, but does the municipality have
to use a portion of *my* tax dollars to rub in the fact that I screwed up
somewhere along the way? Given that at least half the inhabitants of
Woodstock are academics, why not a refined nod in the direction of
Dante, if the repugnant Sartre doesn't get the popular vote? Replace
the offending diamond with a circle (or seven) proclaiming: 'Abandon
hope, all ye who enter here.' If we must be reminded of our mortality
every time we return to hearth and home, let the pasquinade be literate
at the very least.

But road signs don't usually lie. The bottom line is I live in a dead
end. Here reality and metaphor converge. The road rises up gently,
flanked by mature maples and conifers of regal bearing. A big sky sits
atop the leafy parasol; all is tenebrous at the height and in the heavy heat
of a Hoosier summer. Our road is like a thermometer, a straightish tube
with a bulbous base. Drive in and, perforce, two minutes later you drive
out. People come on Sundays especially, and from the air-conditioned
comfort of their silver Camrys ogle our herbaceous borders and living
room curtains. Here, saltbox, country cottage and Californian co-
exist—a happy, largely unostentatious confusion; a herculean Frisbee
throw from the locally hewn, gray and buff limestone of IU. A wise old

humanities professor acquired the land long before we peopled it. He must have laughed all the way to the bank before popping his clogs.

Indiana University may very well be—despite the repeated protestations of wincing administrators—a party school *par excellence*, but my Woodstock has nothing in common with the eponymous, muddy fields of upstate New York where Dylan, Baez, the Byrds and others changed the course of popular music history. There may be dope, nudity, acoustic guitars and a spotty liberteen or two in Woodstock, IN, but you'd never know it. This is a world Virginia Woolf would recognize: 'the postman's knock is heard at eight o'clock, and people go to bed between ten and eleven.' *Epater le bourgeois* is no longer part of our active vocabulary.

Sometimes I wish it were otherwise, but less and less as each thinning year falls away. Tranquility grows on one. Excitement hereabouts is a Labrador barking dementedly, a brace of piston-armed matrons speed walking or the dull, pre-dawn thud of the blue, cellophane-wrapped *H-T* on our immaculately blacktopped driveways. Bloomington may be 'a Midwest gay Mecca,' but this dead end doesn't go in for Sodom and Gomorrah. Unlike medieval Oxford, modern Bloomington can't boast of a Lane of the Seven Deadly Sins. And if we did, the City's Safe and Civil City Program (an egregious waste of public funds) would be down on us like a ton of bricks. We prefer to listen to Moya Andrews delivering her gardening tips in polished Strine on WFIU's 'Focus on Flowers.' In Woodstock, we don't operate on what George Steiner once called 'American time;' the Slow Cities movement has nothing to teach this *barrio*. As a rule, *adagio* is about as fast as it gets, and, if the truth be told, I'm not really complaining. Have I finally gone native; have I finally plumped for *la vie intérieure*? But, remember, this is Bloomington, where watching paint dry can just about make BCAT's coverage of the city council's business seem fast-paced. Slow governance begets slow cities.

In spring, the excitement level ratchets up a notch or two, postponing the need for a dose of transcranial magnetic stimulation. Flotillas of lawnmowers appear, and dandelions, bracken and savannah go the way of all flesh. Jobbing gardeners promise the moon and deliver a wheelbarrow or two of earth. Come fall, the noise level rises further, as platoons of leaf-blowers save us from lumbar pain. To each season its technology: for winter, it's the latest in domestic-scale snowplows and blowers. The chainsaw, however, is no respecter of seasons or Sunday morning lie-ins; it slashes through serenity.

Woodstock is not quite Hemingway's 'wide lawns and narrow minds,' but in truth we incline to reserve not rascality; *le* mow *juste* is our Holy Grail. Cupcakes and candles on the one hand, canines corralled by virtual fences—their bared fangs a magically neutered threat—on the other. Occasionally little gifts are deposited without a word on one's doorstep, a touching insight into our social tentativeness. Year in, year out we activate our rictus smiles and wave to neighbors with whom we have hardly exchanged a word—the roly-poly gays, old Fattypuff and Thinifer (*merci, Monsieur Maurois*), the self-proclaimed 'Wrinklies,' the beldames being walked by their dogs and the desperate housewife with the upturned nose.

Our 'behavioral grammar' and interaction rituals leave something to be desired; on a bad day it's as if we're in a Pinter production. This *petit hameau* is not for glad-handers or serial kissers. If there's a party, we'll all stand around the walls, clenching diet cokes and nibbling our mixed nuts and pitted olives. Wisecrackery is not really our thing, nor is hollering 'Puck Furdue' courtside at Assembly Hall when the Hoosiers are up against the Boiler Makers: decorous discourse is. Here, to quote the exquisite Noël Coward, an actress couldn't get a laugh even 'if she pulled a kipper out of her cunt.' I need hardly say what the neighbors would make of Mr. Coward's ichthyic *aperçu.*

Levity typically takes a backseat to volunteering and genteel political engagement. Our front gardens are festooned with posters when it comes to election time: local judges, school board members, or sheriffs—we all know who the right (wo)man for the job is and our primary colors are staked in the by now jaundiced lawn. The Framers must be high-fiving six feet under as we exercise our democratic rights, the only cost to the community being a temporary blighting of the pristine landscape. I doubt that Camille Paglia ever set foot in Woodstock or its environs, but the good professor surely had something very similar in mind when she spoke of the 'ineffable niceness of Americans.' Here, niceness reigns supreme and blinds us—most of us, most of the time—to the deadness of the end that is nigh. If only that discombobulating sign could be laid to rest, or given a makeover.

I lived in Scotland for six long years before moving to my Midwestern dead end and have not forgotten Samuel Johnson's words: 'The noblest prospect which a Scotchman ever sees, is the high road that leads him to England!' For the last seventeen I have been substituting Hoosier for Scotchman. The separation may be greater, but the sentiment has remained essentially the same. The grass, of course, is always greener on the other side. But these days only just, I must confess. Either my eyesight is failing or my insight is maturing. Bloomington may well be more verdant than I originally thought.

The Daily Divine

'The Middle West was not known for the splendor of its houses of worship...' There's no gainsaying Allan Bloom, but splendor or no splendor, churches are ten a penny in Bloomington. Verily, the houses of God add up to a Potemkin village of heterodox holiness. We are spoiled for spiritual choice: 57 varieties and counting. That I can live with, if push comes to sanctimonious shove. What believers do in their places of worship is not an issue; it's when they feel a need to bear witness in my personal space that I take umbrage. I once heard a commentator on *Newshour* say that Hopper's iconic *Nighthawks* evoked 'a Midwestern kind of loneliness.' Maybe that's one of the factors that drives the natives into the imagined arms of the Almighty. That and a remembrance of Francis Bacon's stern rebuke: 'They that deny a God destroy man's nobility...'

You might be forgiven for thinking that having flooring installed would be a strictly commercial undertaking, but you'd be wrong. The invoice from the *Warehouse Carpet Center* was accompanied by an extensive quotation from the Bible; the blessings of the Lord came with the request for a few thousands dollars. Don't they remember Timothy 6:10: 'For the love of money is the root of all evil'?

The recorded message at *Tonya's Touch* ends with a cheery 'God bless!' Now, cleanliness may be next to godliness, but I don't need God's blessing at that moment, though the good people at the cleaning business evidently feel otherwise: I merely want someone to keep my house spick and span and not fret over the condition of my soul. But that was just the proselytizing *hors d'oeuvre*. One evening I returned to find a pocket diary with 'May God bless you' embossed on the front; another time I was greeted by banana walnut bread (that's what the label said) along with a one-page typed note from Tonya. I quote from it verbatim: 'We are going on a missions trip to the Ukraine. On this trip we will be visiting 7 different orphanages with a total of approximately 850-950 kids. Our goal is to bring each of the children a stocking filled with candy and small toys from McDonalds etc., a wrapped Christmas present (they have never had a wrapped present before), a New Testament bible, and food.' Should I feel disinclined to make a contribution, I am asked to 'at least pray for [the] team.' I need hardly tell you where the blessed banana bread went.

A prescription needs fulfilling, so off one saunters to the local *CVS Pharmacy*. There follows a pleasant exchange with an efficient assistant. I am duly given what I came for, and a little extra. As I am about to pick up my medications, the aforementioned white-coat leans forward and in faintly conspiratorial manner suggests that I join her in fellowship at Bloomington's Unitarian Universalist Church—the UU, as it's affectionately referred to by those in the know. 'Holy cow!' seems like a proportional response, but not a peep emanates from my sagging maw. All I can muster, and that only after a lapse of several seconds, is a feeble 'My soul is beyond redemption.' And then I thought about the Roman Catholic pharmacist fired by Wal-Mart for refusing to fill orders for birth control pills. Should not religion in all its formulations be kept under the counter?

The raging calm of Woodstock on a Wednesday is ruptured by a knock on my front door, which is about as rare an occurrence as a camel passing through the eye of a needle. The God squad: two young men dressed in black trousers and short-sleeved, 50%-polyester, white, button-down shirts. Their uniform is their visiting card: Mormons. 'We have a message for you from Jesus,' they intone, serenely oblivious to the fact that I am watching a program about evangelical madrassas in America, *Jesus Camp*. My evident perplexity in the face of this syntactically uncomplicated sentence does not go unnoticed. They repeat the glad tidings, unfazed.

Maybe Bloomington is no different from the rest of Middle America. After all, 91% of American households own at least one Bible and some 40% of U.S. voters go to church every week, though I am not one of them. Line me up with Homer Simpson: 'I'm having the best day of my life, and I owe it all to not going to Church.' And, contrary to what one might think, not all academics are arrogant atheists or wishy-washy agnostics. According to a just-released survey, some twenty percent of professors at élite American universities say they have no doubt that God exists. With numbers like that, it's hardly surprising that do-gooders occasionally turn up unheralded on one's doorstep, their ten commandments or seven steps to salvation protruding from drooping tote bags. But it gets even better: 20% of Americans believe that the living can communicate with the dead, which is deliciously ironic given George Bush's inability to communicate with the living. Across the Atlantic, secularism seems more deep-rooted: yet another 'recent survey' found that only 3.3% of more than 1,000 Fellows of the Royal Society (the scientific *crème de la crème*) agreed strongly with the statement that 'a personal god exists.'

But the God squad doesn't have it entirely its own way: the University in its secular wisdom recently invited noted philosopher Daniel Dennett, patriarch (along with Richard Dawkins) of the New Atheists, to expound on the cultural and cognitive bases of religious belief. The clear-thinking professor had little time for muddle-headed theism, and the self-selecting audience lapped up his wittily erudite words. Dennett, unlike so many absent-minded professors, is decidedly present in the real world. According to his website, he 'spends most of his summers on his farm in Maine, where he harvests blueberries, hay and timber, and makes Normandy cider wine, when he is not sailing.' Clearly being of this world removes the need to seek out an afterlife.

Given all of this, it is only fitting that the Vatican has finally canonized Indiana's first saint: Blessed Mother Théodore Guérin who—God alone knows why—came years ago from Brittany and founded St. Mary-of-the-Woods College in western Indiana. A student was quoted in the *IDS* as saying that 'becoming a saint is a great thing,' but I don't think the aspiring journalist who wrote the piece intended it to be sardonic. A local pastor was no less eloquent: 'It's really cool. People think of saints long ago and far away, and to have one close to us in Indiana brings it close to home.' In the Hoosier state, I have come to realize, cleanliness and coolness rank next to godliness.

A Night at the Opera

I'm no opera buff, but then Bloomington isn't Bayreuth. Over the years I've dozed decorously in the plush seats of Covent Garden and the Sydney Opera House, to name but two. What a pleasant surprise to discover that similar restorative opportunities are available on this campus and at a tenth of the price: two entire seasons here for the cost of a night in the stalls in London. I would note in passing that the economics of highbrow culture is a burgeoning sub-field of the most dismal of sciences; papers such as 'Why are Covent Garden seat prices so high?'—penned by respected scholars—can be found in the *Journal of Cultural Economics* and make for edifying reading during the intermission.

Does anyone do opera like IU? The 2006-2007 season comprises six full-scale productions, including *Manon*, *Arabella* and *Madama Butterfly*, on top of which there is a ballet season with the evergreen *Nutcracker*. Is there another university in the land with such a spendid operatic history and continuing commitment to this most rarified (and expensive) art form? 'No,' we chorus smugly. Opera is in Bloomington's blood. When

I first hit town, you would be serenaded in Puccini's restaurant by servers who were voice students at IU; I have had tear-jerking arias pour over my linguine, without so much as a 'by your leave.' I was at once astonished and mortified. What do you do when confronted with an award-winning pair of tonsils while dining *à deux*?

Approached from the rear, the Musical Arts Center (MAC in the vernacular) has all the appeal of London's modernist South Bank complex. But things improve if you come at the colossus from the front, where the dourness of the rain-smeared concrete is relieved by slabs of glass and the off-center placement of a stunning Alexander Calder stabile, *Peau Rouge Indiana*. The MAC cannot be compared with Venice's *La Fenice*, but then no one ever said it could or should be. We are grateful for the building we have and count our blessings.

Opening night and the MAC is aglow from within. The apprentice police force, wheeled out more for experience than from necessity, is conducting the traffic with much seriousness of mien and movement. These buzz-cut Barenboims and Bernsteins of the beat have colored lights in lieu of batons, adding to, for want of a better word, the enchantment of the moment. Which brings to mind the (apocryphal?) story of John Cage who, when asked by a journalist if he went to the opera, replied: 'No, I listen to the traffic.'

Don't expect white ties and tails, opera glasses and silver-topped canes, though on a really memorable night you may just espy a few of each. Sir Fopling Flutter is nowhere to be seen and punctilio is in short supply. *Le tout* Bloomington tries its level best, but, with rare exceptions, sartorial heights are not scaled. Even those with dusted-down finery of sorts seem content to partner sequined velvet with black trainers, Brooks Brothers with L.L. Bean. Before the curtain—and what a majestic curtain!—rises, we amble, not altogether comfortably, around the foyer, watching out for colleagues, friends and rivals, silently rehearsing our greetings and *bons mots*, unfortified by at-hand alcohol. Somehow there is never a proper buzz, just a general flatness, so at variance with what is about to transpire on stage. It may be a function of the foyer's brutish design and acoustics, but for whatever reason all sounds of merriment are muffled. Even a matinée at Glynbourne on a squally Sunday makes a gala night at the MAC seem autistic.

If you're thirsty, there's water. No G&T, no bubbly, no liquor of any kind. The mere idea of a crush bar in the Midwest is presumably unimaginable. If there is such a thing as Calvinist opera, this is it. From 7:30 to 11 or later you're on the wagon, unless you've had the foresight to slip a slim hipflask inside your cummerbund or down your bodice. The MAC is no place for the *Inglés borracho*.

The stage sets are spectacular, the costumes a seamstress's delight, the student voices sometimes more than we deserve for the price of admission. I wouldn't term this toy-town opera: the conductor is real and the pit is populated with aspiring, occasionally perspiring, musicians. There are no *claques*, however, and the mightily self-conscious 'Bravos!' leave something to be desired. But the MAC isn't *La Scala,* which means, fortunately, that we don't have to put up with tenor tantrums, such as Roberto Alagna's flouncing off the Milanese stage fed up with the boos and catcalls he received during Franco Zeffirelli's recent production of *Aïda*. Provincialism has its perks.

Sit at the front of the stalls, track the supertitles and you'll need a neck brace next morning. The program is the real thing, glossy, informative and free. When the curtain falls on Act I, I'm like a greyhound out of the trap; the MAC is loo-challenged, so if you are of weak bladder, or have been discretely draining the aforementioned hipflask, you may not want to tarry. Get in quick and you'll miss the *parfum de pee pee*; dither, and you may be re-seated where you don't want to be at the discretion of the management.

My abiding complaint with the world of opera, and this is by no means peculiar to nights at the MAC, is the nervous laughter provoked by the inane antics of supposedly loveable characters such as Leporello. Now, if Shakespeare felt a need for light relief in his tragic plays, who am I to denigrate genre fusion? Still, this is Bloomington and there are more terminal degrees in the audience than conquests on Don Giovanni's list, yet we titter and guffaw at low-grade buffoonery, which, if served up as part of a Christmas pantomime at the London Palladium, would be hissed off stage. Do string theorists and poststructuralists really find this sort of thing amusing? Give me the manic Robin Williams or veteran vaudevillian Ken Dodd when rib tickling is required.

What is it about attending opera, and I'm not just referring to *opera buffa*, that makes us abandon our critical faculties in this way? Why not cut through the amateur dramatics and musical deadwood—*recitativo secco*, for one thing—and get on with the heart-rending love duets, crystal-cracking arias and thumping choruses? That way we could all get out early and hit the bars or hightail it to the Scholars Inn before the parched maestro and performers grab the best tables. Bel canto plus booze equals bliss.

Weighty Matters

'Eat, drink and be merry...' Hoosiers certainly need no encouragement when it comes to the first of these; the pleasures of the table are taken seriously in the Midwest, even if a formal table setting is as perplexing to most Townies and Gownies as Fermat's Last Theorem. That, however, didn't deter the university from inviting Judy 'The Dinner Party' Chicago to spend a not ungenerously remunerated semester in our midst some years ago. The locals scoff their food as if there were no tomorrow; some scoff as if there was no ten minutes later. Mastication is a form of performance art. No wonder universities, IU included, are offering their gormless charges etiquette courses—everyone can now be an Emily Post(er) child.

Indiana may be lagging in the nether regions of the upper quintile of obese states, but we are still hanging in with the real heavyweights. However, the competition is growing, and not just on the home front; 'globesity' has arrived. According to a National Audit Office study, two-thirds of British teenagers are too fat to be soldiers. So, why not simply drop these munitions-like blobs from the bomb bays of B57s over the

Taliban-clogged regions of Waziristan instead of conventional weapons that cause so much collateral damage?

On the smoking front, things are not so grim: Hoosiers had the second highest adult smoking rate among the 50 states in 2005. If we can't stuff ourselves to death, we'll puff ourselves into extinction. That at least seems to be the attitude of our fellow citizens in nearby Bedford, who turned out in force to oppose an official ban on smoking in public places. Bedford is most assuredly not a 'bastion of paleoliberalism,' to use Michael Bérubé's choice term. Here's what the loquacious Charlie Fiddler, a veteran smoker of sixty years, had to say at the local council meeting: 'Well, I don't want to be like Bloomington. Bloomington is a bunch of pot-headed professors, professional students, tree-huggers and people who don't believe in putting an animal to death to save a human. I don't want to be like Bloomington. I want to stay in this town where we have common sense.' Mr. Fiddler doesn't mince his words, unlike so many residents of bijou Bloomington ('shoot' instead of 'shit;' 'Puck Furdue' instead of...). I'm only surprised that he didn't go the whole hog and quote Rudyard Kipling: 'A woman is only a woman, but a good cigar is a smoke.'

Recently and without much forethought, I spent an afternoon in the ER unit of Bloomington Hospital, not as an undercover anthropologist or volunteer caregiver, but as a patient of sorts. I was attended to by a highly competent nurse who, as the afternoon wore on and our inhibitions wore off, revealed his loathing for the grossly obese patients who took up so much of the unit's time and energy. Often, these corn-stuffed, post-ambulatory leviathans can't get into the hospital without a wheelchair and onto the gurney without the aid of a winch, such is their self-induced—and that's the key point—corpulence. No wonder more people are injured by wheelchairs than lawnmowers in the U.S. I'll say one thing for troubled, C-list celebrity Nicole Richie: she can be hoisted onto the waiting bed with the flick of a paramedic's wrist. But not these Hoosier hulks. In the words of a *Spectator* columnist, 'Fat Americans are old hat. What's more striking is the complete confidence with which they carry their fatness.' Soon all public spaces, from theater seats (Broadway is embracing gourmet snacking, much to the consternation of the performers who are drowned out by the continuous munching, crunching and slurping of the gourmands in the stalls) to park benches, will need to be re-calibrated to accommodate the needs of an expanding majority. It's already happening in the domestic sphere.

The last time I bought a house, friends inquired immediately as to the square footage, not the location of the *stanza d'amore* ('love room'). I hadn't the faintest idea. One would never be asked such a question in the U.K., let alone know the answer. But here space matters, more it seems, than architectural design, building materials, or the tastefulness of the décor. The *aula magna* of the university has found its equivalent in the 'great room' of the modern, middle-class home. These cavernous spaces, somewhere between aircraft hanger and barn, are accessorized with massive couches, jumbo-sized plasma screens and crescents of button-backed, leather recliners designed to accommodate the fuller-bodied American weaned on Big Macs and ferried around by over-sized SUVs. As the nation's tummies inflate, the average new house has grown from 1,950 square feet in 1990 to 2,227 in 2005. Parkinson's Law of Personal Space?

One of the things we do well in universities is reflect on, occasionally even engage with, the world-as-is. Given the significant rise in obesity in recent years (66% of Americans are overweight; 32% obese), it's hardly surprising that the academy has latched onto the subject of fatness; it's the latest addition to the roster of advocacy programs—women's studies, queer studies, etc. Predictably, sub-editors are having a field day: 'Fat studies gaining weight in academia' is how the *Daily Pennsylvanian* led

off. The *New York Times* was more restrained: 'Big People on Campus.'
But with courses such as 'Social Construction of Obesity' and 'Fat
and Society,' books entitled *Revolting Bodies* and *Tipping the Scales of
Justice,* and a conference 'Fat and the Academy' (FATA) hosted by Smith
College, one should not be surprised.

Kathleen LeBesco, a pioneer in the field of flesh, had the misfortune
to lose 70 lbs. over the course of a semester or two. If you're an apostle for
fat studies, relative thinness can create serious difficulties: 'I'm worried
that losing weight is going to kill my credibility as a scholar.' This
breathtaking statement issued from the mouth of a professor and was
reported without ridicule by the *Chronicle of Higher Education.* Should
those who lecture on male pattern baldness look like Yul Brynner;
should those who teach about AIDS have been afflicted themselves with
the disease? Time for Ms. LeBesco to re-read Plato. If this is an indicator
of the intellectual rigor associated with the putative 'multi-disciplinary
field of Fat Studies,' then we should be worried. Flab is bad enough;
but flabby scholarship is—dare I say it?—the thin end of the wedge.

Rites and Wrongs of Passage

Once upon a time I was a schoolboy. There were teachers and pupils in a school, located on school grounds. Later I went to university, where I mixed with fellow students on campus. I graduated from university and embarked on an academic career, an aspiring scholar, a would-be professor. Pupil, student, scholar, professor. Life was simple, language clear. No more.

My son, in high school, is a student (not a pupil) on a campus (not school grounds) taught by a faculty (not school teachers). He will likely attend something ghastly called a prom and graduate garbed in purple, because that is what one does. Actually, it is what one does at middle and junior high schools, too. I don't get it.

Schools have dictionaries. Why don't administrators—or, to employ an abominable neologism, educators—use them more often? A pupil is not a student is not a scholar. It's all so achingly pretentious and, ultimately, damaging. Schools do not need to appropriate the terminology of universities (and is it only Americans who routinely refer to university as school?) and colleges or ape their rituals; they should develop their own protocols. Schools are schools; places where children are taught and learn. School*children* are just that. Why deny them their childhood? Why catapult them into adulthood? The rituals and attire of graduation have evolved over the centuries, and are an important symbolic component of university life. They have no place in the school system. Imitation may be the sincerest form of flattery, but this is sincerity we can do without.

What's happening in the nation's schools is part of a broader, pernicious trend. Dressing our pubescent offspring in tuxedos and ball-gowns and sending them off to proms in stretch limousines before wrapping them in plastic graduation robes makes one think of six-year old JonBenet Ramsey and the meretricious sub-culture of 'Little Miss' beauty pageants—Indiana has a Miss Indiana Princess competition for those of you with daughters who are second or third graders—wickedly satirized in the movie *Little Miss Sunshine*. The murder of this child cast the spotlight on a penumbral world populated by young girls, wannabe Marilyns or Madonnas, egged on by single-minded parents. The language used by the media to describe JonBenet said it all: 'a painted baby, a sexualized toddler beauty queen.' It is a mystery to me why parents encourage this cruel loss of innocence; equally, I am perplexed that our society, at once so enlightened and puritanical, can tolerate the unabashed sexualization of young girls. It's surely time for another movie, *Little Missogyny*.

But one shouldn't be surprised, given how the nation's school system has apparently embarked on a muddle-headed mission to eradicate childhood and all the symbolic accoutrements thereof. The goal of the current generation of dreary 'educrats' is to make our kids think they are grown-ups long before their minds and bodies have matured. If we dress them like adults and label them adults, they'll behave like adults. Don't take my word for it; just look at the statistical data relating to

teenage pregnancies, drug consumption and gun use. Even in idyllic
Bloomington, childhood is being subverted. As J.B. Priestly said: 'Like
its politicians and its wars, society has the teenagers it deserves.'

And what happens when these young adults arrive on campus?
They booze in frat houses and fornicate in dorms with the fervor of
the born-again. And what does Auntie IU do? Nothing much as a rule,
apart from an occasional crackdown followed by a public denunciation
of underage drinking delivered by the long-suffering Dean of Students.
Of course, there's not much anyone can do, human nature being what
it is. Dope and coke (I'm sure these terms are frightfully dated) are
inescapable ingredients of the contemporary undergraduate experience,
which is only to be expected, given that they are commonplaces of high
school life in Bloomington.

Come finals, however, the university behaves as if it were a
helicopter parent, and resorts to well intentioned if infantilizing
behavior. Dorms are plastered with notices telling all and sundry that
it is 'Quiet week.' The massed faculty and administrative ranks of the
College of Arts and Sciences, led by their smiling dean, don logo-
bearing aprons to serve hot food late at night in the lobby of the Main
Library to the presumptively malnourished student body, as if these
substance-sampling teens couldn't rustle up a plate of beans and rice
for themselves.

Also at this time, parents receive from the Residence Halls
Association a letter suggesting that they purchase a 'care package' to
help their child 'through the rigors of final exams.' On offer are the
Hoosiers Spirit care package, the Fruit Basket Pack and the Exam
Survival Kit, along with a pre-scripted greeting card: 'While you're
thinking about finals, somebody is thing about you.' In that case, a line
of 'happy dust' would be many kids' first thought. All this for progeny
who are old enough to don condoms, mount motorbikes, vote for Pat

Robertson and enlist in the military. Shouldn't we have treated them as kids while they were at school and shouldn't we treat them as adults now that they are at university?

Talented Totty

For slow-loading pulchritude you can't beat the *Miss Indiana University* website with its curlicued lettering and salmon pink background. Here you'll meet the contestants for the 2006 Miss IU Pageant, the first, for reasons that escape me, to have been held for almost four decades. You'll learn about the organizing body, whose stated goal is to redefine 'the Miss America tradition in a unique way that epitomizes the great city of Bloomington.' There is a list of sponsors, which, to my surprise, includes the IU Foundation. So, that's where donors' unrestricted dollars go...

A dozen lovelies competed for the crown. To be in with a chance you should be 'a unique young woman who is an involved citizen and campus role model' and you absolutely must have a platform issue, be it saving whales or feeding the destitute of Darfur. There is nothing in the promotional literature about having perfect teeth and a near perfect body, yet the dozen finalists seemed possessed of both. It must be the Lake Wobegon effect, for here all bosoms are above average amplitude. I thought of Susanna Paasonen's observation that beauty pageants are 'sites for defining racial and national ideals, normative measurements, shapes, and colors of womanhood.' The local ideal hasn't strayed far from the Aryan archetype, that's for sure.

Certainly, it was hard not to notice the winner's embonpoint; her shimmering evening gown was slashed almost to the navel. This may not matter, formally, as far as the IU competition is concerned, but the winner of this pageant automatically proceeds to the Miss Indiana and thence, if successful a second time, to the Miss America pageant, for both of which swimwear is *de rigueur*—as is, by implication, a near flawless body. These gals sure as hell do not have what the foppish Karl Lagerfeld called 'skinny bones;' all are wholesome and none is likely to land a role as an extra in the stage production of *Schindler's List*.

But these are ladies to be reckoned with; they are blessed with talents of a kind that one can but dream of: Kelli Dove's specialty is *ballet en point*, her sister Erin's is stomp dance (*ballet en rage?*) and the sweetly named Jasmine Beams plays viola. But the title went to the praeternaturally self-assured Miss Betsy Uschkrat, a voice student at the Jacobs School of Music who wowed the judges with an aria from *La Bohème*. Betsy, whose surname would challenge a *Scrabble* champion, is not to be found buried in the third row of the chorus; she played the lead in last season's *Roméo et Juliette* and will also star in an upcoming production of *Manon*. This young lady has genuine talent and a social conscience: she founded *Heart and Soul Indiana* and has been named the state spokesperson for *Feeding Indiana's Hungry*. On top of this, she has a smile that would light up Dunn Meadow in darkest December. It's hardly surprising, though of questionable taste, that the Music School's display ads carry the text: 'An opera by Jules Massenet featuring Miss Indiana Betsy Uschkrat...'

Having swept the boards in the 'great' city of Bloomington she took her talents to the even greater city of Indianapolis and repeated the story. Right now she's focused on the ultimate dream, the 2007 Miss America pageant, for which she'll be wearing a strapless emerald green dress which is in her words 'not too poofy.' Betsy told the *Indiana Daily Student* that she 'will be working out a lot to get that swimsuit body exactly how I like it for the swimsuit competition.' The IU family (see my jeremiad 'Family Affairs') is holding its collective breath. It's a pity Betsy didn't hold hers a little longer: 'It will be like nothing I nor anyone else has ever known before,' she burbled to the *IDS* reporter. Betsy may be a diva-in-the-making, but she's no orator, that's for sure, but, then, oratory is not a talent that is much valued these days in academe.

I think I now understand that roadside billboard—the postmodern embodiment of the traditional *os academicum* (university orator; academic mouth, literally)—on the road to Indianapolis shrieking that 'IU IS HOT,' though I'm not sure that John Henry Cardinal Newman would fully understand what ball gowns and billboards have to do with higher education, or why the cover of the latest faculty telephone directory is emblazoned with the imbecilic slogan 'IU is RED HOT.'

Mollycoddling

The customer is always right. Heaven forfend that this notion should take root in the groves of academe. Unfortunately, use of the term 'customer' for 'student' has already become altogether too common Students may pay their way but that does not mean they know what is good for them. Call me old fashioned, but the title of professor means that one, in fact, professes. In Britain it is still the assumption (certainly in ancient universities) that when one is appointed to a chair (in philosophy, mathematics or whatever) one speaks *ex cathedra*, that is to say, with sapiental and positional authority ('crystallized charisma,' to quote from William Clark's monumental *Academic Charisma and the Origins of the Research University*). In short, students should heed their professors.

Young and sometimes not so young minds attend universities to learn—when they're not playing lacrosse or flipping burgers, that is. They learn primarily from their professors, the anointed experts in a given domain. This relationship is most simply, if unfashionably, characterized as that of master and apprentice, and Romantically

enacted in weekly tutorials, accompanied by cake and Madeira. It is
rather different from the relationship between a customer and, say, a
storeowner or parking valet. But such a characterization is, apparently,
passé. For good or ill, the sage on the stage is being superceded by the
guide on the side, while card-carrying social constructivists at IU and
elsewhere prattle on about 'zones of proximal development' to anyone
who'll listen.

Today's students at 'Bubblegum University' see themselves as
shoppers buying dollops of education (three credits of this, one of
that) just as they purchase DVDs or groceries—'atomized individuals
making a personal choice in the marketplace to maximize their economic
power,' as Jeffrey Williams put it in a perspicacious essay, *The Pedagogy
of Debt*—and are encouraged in this perverse practice by the actions of
complicit administrators and fearful professors. Students believe they
know what they need, and expect to be provided with a syllabus that
is to their liking and a teaching style that makes them feel 'respected as
an individual.' The *IDS* quotes an IU senior on the matter: 'If I don't
like a particular professor, I think of ways all semester that I can say
things in the evaluation.' As Oscar Wilde declared: 'There is no sin
except stupidity.'

Once or twice I have invoked George Steiner—'the nearest we
had to a Guru Don,' according to Arianna Stassinopoulos Huffington,
Cambridge graduate and blogger *extraordinaire*—at the university
commencement ceremony: 'A worthwhile university or college is quite
simply one in which the student is brought into personal contact with,
is made vulnerable to, the aura and threat of the first-class.' I'm only
surprised I wasn't yanked off the platform in full view of our scandalized
customers and their loved ones for exhibiting such crass élitism. With
hindsight I could just as well have quoted Herman B Wells, who, on
the occasion of his inauguration as President of Indiana University,

said that the university was a place where 'students learn the slow and arduous processes of mental discipline.' Sadly, the likes of Steiner and Wells belong to a dying breed. These days pie-in-the-sky idealism has been replaced by pie-in-the-face pragmatism. I have just learned that the dean of the Kelley Business School and seven of his professorial colleagues have agreed to be pied (*sic*) in the face by students as part of a fundraising event.

Over the course of the last sixteen years I have read literally hundreds of student evaluations. I should point out that the survey instrument we use has about as much construct validity as a roll of toilet paper; the battery of questions is designed to solicit students' likes and dislikes, rather than to determine what educrats like to call the 'quality of the educational experience' or 'learning outcomes.' The process has been described by one of my colleagues as a 'product satisfaction survey.' She is too polite by half.

Now, there are good teachers, bad teachers and some great teachers. We know who they are, and they probably know it themselves. Whenever I read banalities such as 'professor X is hot,' 'professor Y's reading list is too long,' or 'professor Z did not give me enough eye contact,' I am not sure whether to laugh or cry. But at least I'm not a lone wolf howling at the lunacy of the situation. Harvey Mansfield, reflecting on his many years at Harvard, excoriates the limitations of the customer-centric model of higher education: 'Course evaluations by students... undermine the authority of professors. They make professors accountable to students on the basis of needing to please them, like businesses pleasing customers or elected officials pleasing voters. The superiority of those who know over those who don't is slighted, and the students' judgment comes down to the charm of the professor as students perceive it.' Well said, Sir!

The fetishization of course evaluations and the inflated role they have been granted in annual reviews and salary setting exercises have had a corrosive effect on both faculty morale and academic standards. Student evaluations have become tools for demeaning professors and dumbing down the classroom experience. They give voice to those whose voices should be muted; those who, in the words of Piers Paul Read, are still trapped in 'the swamp of their own immaturity.' The pettiness and vindictiveness all too often revealed in student evaluations demonstrate how debased the exercise has become. Web-based faculty rating schemes (RateMyProfessors.com, MyProfessorSucks.com) and social networking services (Facebook.com) have exacerbated this lamentable trend. Those students most likely to post comments (not to mention photos or video of their professors) are, as one might expect, those who have something negative or *ad hominem* to say. I have looked at a few of these online sites and am appalled at the selectivity and spitefulness of what is to be found. No wonder some professors have resorted to litigation in an effort to protect their reputations; others, not surprisingly, boost their own scores with bogus entries (equivalent to reputation gaming on eBay). The lunatics are running the asylum.

You know the old Shavian saw: 'He who can, does; he who cannot, teaches.' In academe, it runs thus: 'He who can, teaches; he who cannot, administers.' As the population of suits grows at a rate much faster than the full-time faculty, make-work needs to be found for the sprawling ranks of assistant-, associate-, and vice-this-that-and-the-other: the original Parkinson's Law. What better than to create a mini-bureaucracy devoted to classroom civility and the like as a way to soak up some of the surplus labor?

I've taught on both sides of the Atlantic and I have never felt a need to consult or cite a so-called civility code. Apparently, our customers have the idea that a classroom is a cross between a playground and a cafeteria. Moreover, they seem to feel that since they help pay the professor's mortgage, it is they who should determine what kinds of behaviors and pedagogy will be tolerated. Instead of simply booting out unruly elements, giving them a failing grade, or rusticating them, the system (and I include IU in my cavalier indictment) in its wisdom has come up with a wheeze to ensure that more administrative posts are created without, at the same time, entirely alienating our cherished customers: civility codes. These are sometimes discussed under the rubric of campus climate. I'll spare you the many vogue definitions of the concept; simply consult the bibliography of campus climate reports hosted on the website of the National Consortium of Directors of LGBT (Lesbian, Gay, Bisexual and Transgender) Resources in Higher Education for a flavor of current thinking.

I examined a few of these codes myself and was dumbfounded. The syllabus for a computing course at a university in North Carolina included the following: 'Turn off your cell phone before class starts... Don't read the newspaper during class...Don't listen to electronic or audio equipment during class...No prolonged conversations during class.' Why would anyone want do any of the above while attending class? One knows how to behave in class, and if one doesn't, one shouldn't be attending class in the first place. Perhaps I am being naïve. Another IU senior was quoted in the *IDS*: 'I'm a slacker sometimes and space off in class...network with my friends in class.' How things have changed.

'Shut up, I'm talking to my mom,' was how one typically self-absorbed teenager at the McKinney North High School in Texas—center of a recent, much publicized cheerleading scandal—responded to her teacher when instructed to stop chatting on her cell phone in class. However, all is not yet lost: Cynthia Frisby, an associate professor at the University of Missouri, doesn't beat about the digital bush:

'Anyone who engages in rude, thoughtless, selfish behavior, such as use of a cellphone for instant messages, games, etc., will have his or her cellphone confiscated…and be excused from the class.' Texas high schools take note.

If university administrators hadn't been so diffident about reading the riot act in recent years and were less concerned with placating their narcissistic customers, we would never have reached this point. Make students accept responsibility for their own actions or face the consequences, and to hell with the idiocies of climate management. Leave such to the heating engineers.

Semper Fidelis

You can tie the knot on campus, provided you book well in advance. Beck Chapel ('A still point in a turning world,' as my decanal colleague Patrick O'Meara, quoting one T.S. Eliot, characterized it) abuts a small dry-stone walled graveyard, replete with the remains of privileged Binkleys, Dunns and Huttons, a mere yard or two from the Indiana Memorial Union ('Your choice for destination weddings at IU'), where, if devoid of imagination or heaving with uncontainable lust, or both, you could spend your *luna de miel*.

The non-denominational chapel (Bible, Torah, Koran on tap), with its limestone exterior, lich gate, slate roof, honey-colored oak pews, stained glass windows and small organ, hosts more than 100 weddings a year. For a modest $300 you can have this 'still point' for three hours, plus Bach, or whatever music takes your matrimonial fancy, played by a live organist, a doctoral student from the Jacobs School of Music. Throughout the year this tiny place of worship is open to anyone seeking a moment's respite from the pressures of contemporary academic life or simply wishing to commune with their

Maker. This is neither high church nor Heathrow airport chapel, but it nonetheless meets a need in none too shabby fashion and has done so for half a century: the first couple, a William and a Mary, were married while the chapel was still under construction. If you want something flashier, then why not hire the high-ceilinged, marble-floored space of the IU Auditorium foyer for both your wedding ceremony and reception? Where else can you say 'I do' beneath an extravaganza of Thomas Hart Benton paintings, part of the Indiana Murals series? For the record, the heavily mustachioed Benton was influenced by El Greco and, implausible though it might seem, taught Jackson Pollock; Benton, a self-declared 'enemy of modernism,' had no time for Abstract Expressionism, which, I suppose, goes to show. I'll have more to say on Benton's work and its reception locally later.

On the other hand, if pink is your favorite color and you fancy your post-nuptials in a more rustic setting, then point the throaty Camaro in the direction of the Abbey Inn, home to the 60-seat Brown County Indiana Wedding Chapel (an antique store in a previous incarnation), on the fringes of Nashville and a mere stone's throw from the Little Nashville Opry, local provider of 'Foot Stompin Fun.' This may be just what the doctor or your psychosexual therapist ordered. The inn, and I have no reason to believe otherwise, is a 'very unique lodging establishment...with minimal staff.' The entwined hearts above the entrance cleverly differentiate it from Beck Chapel and alert the would-be bride and groom as to what lies in store. The Abbey Inn and Beck Chapel are at once eighteen and a million miles apart.

According to the inn's website there is no elevator: 'Customers of size should be aware that all beds and all hot tubs have weight limits. Cardiologists suggest that patients who are taking beta-blockers or ACE inhibitors...should use hot tubs cautiously.' Customers of size!

In this neck of the woods, that's presumably the bulk of their clientele. Here the wedding package includes the minister, flowers, unity candle, music and dubious-sounding 'videography'.

Still, if you're gonnna peg out while making out after your nuptials, where better than leafy Brown County? I doubt, though, that many Gownies beat a path to the Abbey Inn, but perhaps there are some closet Country & Western aficionados in our cerebral ranks (*The* Stanley Fish is a self-confessed fan of classic C&W lyrics: 'If I said you had a beautiful body would you hold it against me?') who have pledged troth in this homage to kitsch before line dancing across State Road 46 to listen to Bobby Bare or Tanya Tucker regurgitate their greatest hits.

And so to option #3, in which the mountain comes to Mohammed, unlike the Abbey Inn where the mountain apparently comes to the hot tub. A former colleague decided that her particular knot should be tied in the back garden. Decorations were erected, close friends invited and the requisite finery donned. Under a makeshift trellis, the wedding officiant read the time-honored words, the couple responded in time-honored fashion and the deal was sealed. Being of another era, I had no idea that the matrimonial experience could be customized and home-delivered, like pizza. But this is the holy Hoosier state where there's stiff competition for your bridal bucks, as a quick Google search makes clear. The following is typical of the customer-focused approach: 'I perform contemporary, casual, or traditional nondenominational weddings primarily in Indiana & Kentucky. 7 days per week—including holidays. $200 for wedding and rehearsal. Location & travel may increase fees. Will travel to the location of your choice.' Impulsive romantics take note.

It is hard, however, not to feel that the sacramental is being sacrificed at the altar of sloth. The term 'marriage of convenience' is taking on a new meaning in the heartland, but we're still trailing Las Vegas, which offers the ultimate in ceremonial convenience, the drive-through wedding. 'Tis surely but a matter of time…

Naming Mania

Sandwich (after the earl) and Wellington boot (after the duke) are staples of the English language, but you won't find a Sandwich or Wellington University in the Sceptred Isle. Birmingham, Edinburgh, Manchester, Sheffield are all names of notable red brick universities (equivalent to major public research universities in the U.S.). British universities usually inherit the name of their host metropolis. It's not terribly imaginative, but at least it makes sense and helps spatially challenged students. As the man who granted me admission to academia, Professor Sir Graham Hills, put it: 'No city or town could regard itself as arrived without a university to add to its cathedral, town hall and play house.' In the interests of historical accuracy, however, I should acknowledge that several Oxbridge colleges (e.g., Balliol, Merton) assumed the name of their founder or benefactor, while others, as once was commonplace, are named after saints.

Place-based naming is also the norm here, but is by no means always the case or always intuitive: perplexingly, the University of Indiana is located in Pennsylvania. Cornell, Duke, Harvard, Rockefeller,

Stanford, Vanderbilt and Yale are just some of the lustrous private institutions that bear the name of their magnanimous founder and testify to the desire of robber barons and others to see their name outlast their mortal remains. And then there's Bob Jones University, about which the less said the better. No other country can match the United States when it comes to philanthropy, and few other sectors attract donations the way higher education does. It is surely only a matter of time before a Dell or Trump University is established. But I wouldn't bet on Woody Allen joining the trend, for it was he who said, memorably: 'I don't want to achieve immortality through my work. I want to achieve it by not dying.'

The top-ten private universities in this country likely out-perform the top-twenty universities (public or private) of every other country on earth. If your liquid assets don't quite stretch to creating a university *de novo*, there is no shortage of naming alternatives. You can badge a college or school, or, in an effort to save a few millions, have your name affixed to a building, deanship, chair, professorship, fellowship or scholarship. The options are limited only by the imagination of those well meaning if oleaginous types who work in the euphemistically labeled world of institutional advancement.

Walk around the Bloomington campus with your gaze directed both overhead and downward and you will be amazed by the number of already named and potentially nameable elements to be found, ranging from buildings and benches to red paving bricks. There's the Lilly Library (named after the family-founded pharmaceutical firm that gave us Prozac, a product enjoyed by the nonagenarian Ruth Lilly, the sole living heiress to the family fortune), Neal-Marshall Black Culture Center (the campus white elephant, named after the first IU African-American male and female graduates), Herman B Wells Library (self-explanatory; a building described charitably by blurber Gubar as 'venerable in size, if not in grace'), Bryan Hall (baptized, appropriately, in honor of the university's longest-serving president) and Kirkwood Observatory (after a professor of astronomy, known in his day as the 'Kepler of America'). I've trodden on more people on my way into the IMU than I've had hot dinners at Truffles, though most of the names underfoot mean nothing to me—the Burns family has a cluster of fourteen bricks, their individual names still legible. And who was, or is, Katharine R. Doerbaum, a lone brick in this isthmus of baked red letters?

Naming can take other forms; our pretty campus is bedecked with trees, shrubs and seats named in loving memory of a deceased colleague, alumnus or friend of IU: there's a Pink Flowering Dogwood dedicated to one James Gaylord Hart, a former professor of Religious Studies, that catches the eye and, of course, Tuck Langland's captivating sculpture of the Great Man. My favorite spot is the calming space bounded tightly by the Collegiate Gothic of Morrison, Goodbody, Sycamore and Memorial Halls, through which the short Philosopher's Path weaves. Here a concrete bench, a memorial to Hector-Neri Casteñada ('Professor, Colleague, Friend') chills the butt but warms the memory. Is there, I wondered, an inventory of all those whose names are speckled for one reason or another across the campus? Who, more to the point, would undertake such a pointless prosopography?

The IU business school is now known as the Kelley School, named after the entrepreneur who founded Steak 'n Shake. I was seated but two tables away at a black-tie dinner when the spotlight was turned (literally) on Mr. Kelley and family to announce his $23.5 million gift to the university. I had never been so close to Croesus. One thought preoccupied me during the remainder of the gala event: how many cows must have been slaughtered, how many burgers grilled, for the benevolent Mr. Kelley to have amassed a fortune of such proportions that he could donate far more money to IU in one evening than IU would have to pay me for several lifetimes' work? But Kelley is not alone. Some $40 million or so guaranteed that the Jacobs family name would play on and on in Bloomington. Other schools will surely follow Business and Music along this route; egotism and largesse are a marriage made in tax-deductible heaven.

At the next level down the donation chain come named chairs and professorships. Endowed professorships are nothing new; Henry VIII set the ball rolling when he established a number of Regius professorships in the mid-sixteenth century. Today, corporations and wealthy individuals have taken the place of monarchs, but I find it hard to mention the Regius Professorship of Moral and Pastoral Theology or the Bywater and Sotheby Professor of Byzantine and Modern Greek Language and Literature at Oxford University in the same breath as—and, no, this is not parody—the Enron Chair in Risk Management at the Jesse H. Jones Graduate School of Management at Rice University. Now, there you have a nominal triple-decker: Enron (chair), Jones (school), Rice (university). It doesn't get any better (or more long-winded) in the naming game.

The oldest university professorships at IU are those named after James H. Rudy. They were established a mere 500 or so years after Henry VIII's professorships. A Rudy isn't a Regius, but I was mightily pleased to be anointed a Rudy professor a decade ago. Predictably, my curiosity got the better of me and I enquired as to the nature of the endowment. I sometimes wish that I hadn't. It turns out that Rudy's estate was gifted to the university on his death. Rudy's wife Virginia, I discovered courtesy of the University Archives, shot and killed their three children before turning the gun on herself. A few years later, James used the same gun to blow his brains out while abed. But, then, Henry VIII was no saint either.

Pompous, *Moi?*

'Care to order, guys?' This from the mouth of a teenage waitress in the Limestone Grille, a relatively upscale restaurant by Bloomington standards. She was addressing yours truly and the late Tom Sebeok, Distinguished Professor of Semiotics at Indiana University. Tom was approaching his eightieth birthday; I had passed the half-century mark. I glanced at Tom; he chuckled, too kind to say or do anything. Our server—to use the politically correct label—evidently had no sense of the inappropriateness of her preferred form of address. Had we been a couple of twenty-something jocks I might have understood, but our demeanor, manners, conversation and ages were about as far removed from jockdom as one could imagine. I was perplexed, and not for the first or last time. Years on, I am as appalled as ever by the liberties that total strangers take with one.

What, I wondered, was wrong with 'gentlemen,' a universally understood and socially appropriate term? 'Guys' was not just a hopelessly inexact appellation given our combined age, but one that implied a degree of familiarity that certainly did not exist. Perhaps servers believe that superficial familiarity translates into more generous gratuities. Regrettably, familiarity is no longer earned in this country; it is simply taken for granted by all and sundry. Unlike Bono, Cher, and Sting I have two names (is The Donald one or two?) that I use commonly: 'Blaise' and 'Cronin.' Call me reactionary or self-important, or both, but I expect those whom I have not met previously, or who are mere acquaintances, to use the latter, preferably preceded by a 'Mr.,' 'Dr.,' or 'Professor.' The use of 'Blaise' is something one works up to, gradually and graciously. How would our *savoir faire*-challenged server survive in France, where one has to navigate routinely between '*tu*' and '*vous*' with all the potential pitfalls?

Don't get me wrong, I am not advocating that we adopt the rigid protocols that have characterized the German workplace (bowing and clicking heels in front of *Herr doktor doktor Jahnke;* always referring to one's female colleague as '*Frau Merkel*'), but some controls on excessive familiarity are in order. I do not take kindly to intrusive telemarketers addressing me as 'Blaise'—though more often than not it's 'Blasé'—nor realtors within ten seconds of a first handshake exercising a familiarity I would only accept from my chums. I do not want adolescents or hucksters of any stripe believing that they have the right to speak to me as if I were their friend. I do not want my hairdresser—unless her name is Claire and she was mentioned in *Bloomington Days*—or anyone else bawling out my first name in a salon or other public space. I want a modicum of respect. The occasional 'Sir' or 'M'am' (I'll take either) can go a long way.

Egalitarianism is all very well, but should not be used as an excuse for transgressive social behaviors. As it happens, we are generally very aware of the need not to intrude on one another's personal space, and the physical separation between two conversing Americans will typically be greater than in most other cultures. Given this well documented fact, it is puzzling that there are no comparable constraints operating in the discursive domain. Which naturally brings us to the classroom. I was taken aback the first time a student at IU with whom I had never had so much as a passing exchange referred to me as 'Blaise' in the lecture theater. In fairness I should confess that my early days in the U.K., being at the time an uncritical fan of A.S. Neill and Summerhill, I had tried to be hip by having my students call me by my first name, but that resulted in a phony sense of friendship and caused problems when contentious disciplinary or grading issues arose. I quickly reverted to type.

There is, or should be, a separation between students and professors. Of course, things may change when one develops a close working relationship with a doctoral student, but in the classroom I make it clear that I expect to be addressed formally (i.e., with a 'Mr.,' 'Dean,' or whatever in front of the 'Cronin' bit). I, for my part, now ask each of my students how they would like to be addressed, and most (actually, all to date) have settled for first names. When I was an undergraduate in Dublin my professors addressed me as 'Mr. Cronin.' As a teenager it felt somewhat strange to be spoken to by one's elders and betters in such fashion, though, to be honest, I rather enjoyed it. But that was then.

Today almost anything goes. Ben Yagoda wrote a piece in the *Chronicle of Higher Education* on contemporary name-calling in academia, noting that the multiplicity of student sub-cultures on campuses across the nation translates into a hodge-podge of local practices. He also highlighted the fact that some female professors find a formal title helpful in establishing respectful relationships and dealing with boundary issues.

When I visit my dentist I am happy to address him as doctor in recognition of his professionally validated (and invariably framed) achievements—have you noticed the plaque on the surgery wall? By the same token, I don't see why my equally hard earned credentials shouldn't be acknowledged. Senators, judges and doctors don't have a monopoly on titular propriety. What's good for these professional geese is surely good for the professorial gander.

And now a brief coda. In 1999 I entered into an extended e-mail exchange with the sociologist Robert Merton. I had drawn upon his work since I was a doctoral student, and had always been in awe of his erudition, though we never met. When, during our correspondence, he asked if he could be granted 'the privilege of *tutoiment*,' and then moved in the space of a few emails from 'Dear Dean Cronin' through 'Dear Blaise' to 'My very dear Blaise' I was touched, but—and this is the pertinent part—I could not bring myself to reciprocate in like fashion. I found it impossible to address the distinguished octogenarian other than as 'Dear Professor Merton' or 'Dear RKM.' Anything else would have seemed crassly inappropriate.

As I reflect on the unconscious discourtesy of the Bloomington server, a trivial instance, I readily concede, of an accelerating national disposition to promiscuous informality in social interaction, I sometimes wonder if I am living in the wrong century and/or wrong continent. Who was it that said, 'A prig is a fellow who is always making you a present of his opinions'?

Nature Red in Tooth and Claw

You go to Indianapolis zoo, pay your $13.50 and gawp guiltily at the animals in their cages, pens, pits and tanks. Who knows, if you're an empty nester, you may even wish to adopt an African elephant or poxy panda to make yourself feel good.

In Woodstock Place the tables are turned, for it is we who are the watched: inverse panopticism. Our modernist house with its walls of glass is a fine thing—the dialectic between Californian interior and luxuriant exterior (think of a Henri Rousseau painting) is a source of constant pleasure—but with the wrap-around flora comes an ark's worth of fauna. We may be well within the city limits, but someone seems not to have told the local population of quadrupeds; deer, foxes, raccoons, squirrels, possums and chipmunks roam over yard and drive as if civilization was still a decade or two around the corner. And don't rule out the possibility of a big cat—by which I assuredly don't mean an over-fed tabby—fetching up on your doorstep: such has, indeed, happened in Bloomington's environs. I guess this is what is meant by *rus in urbe.* St. Francis would have traded Assisi for Bloomington in a flash.

Recently, I stepped onto the patio and found myself thirty feet from three recumbent deer, positioned as if in a Busby Berkeley routine, all six forelegs forward in perfect alignment. I stared wide-eyed, as did they, nostrils twitching—theirs, not mine. As I reached for my camera, the trio rose as one and vaulted in balletic fashion over the perimeter fence. The moment had passed. But there have been others; the record is a mesmerizing and mesmerized group of eight on the front lawn. I've since learned that our faces are like beacons to deer, beacons that need to be dimmed: hence the faintly ridiculous deerstalker (a.k.a. Sherlock Holmes) hat worn in the Scottish Highlands.

For every buck or doe there's a dozen bushy-tailed squirrels. From afar these upper branch trapeze artists are a delight to watch; closer to home and in the dead of night their charm quotient plummets. Cute critters are anything but cute when their rooftop scampering ruptures one's REM sleep stage. By 2 a.m. I'm wondering why BB guns aren't standard issue to Bloomingtonians. A wildlife expert revealed recently that there had been six squirrel attacks on humans in as many months in North Dakota. I do hope Hoosier squirrels are better behaved. But things can get even worse: enter raccoons. These brutish beasts are to red squirrels as sumo wrestlers are to bantamweights. Scamper becomes thunder and lust for a BB gun metastasizes into a craving for a Remington Magnum.

Leading the local cuteness stakes is a palm-sized chipmunk, five dashing black stripes arching along its furry length: he has all the elements of a miniature Davy Crockett hat-in-the-making. Chippy inhabits a crevice in the wall outside my study window. Come the sun, come Chippy. This teensy weensy Parkinsonian packet with its basilisk stare soaks up the rays like a Brit in Benidorm, oblivious to my brooding presence behind the glass. When not getting his daily fix of vitamin D, my companion Chippy is busy re-creating the catacombs of Rome beneath the front lawn with, of course, more than a little help from his extended family. One day my world will cave in, literally.

A few yards away sits the tiny, unblinking toad which has taken up residence in the miniscule pond. And where did it come from and how did it know to settle here of all places? The local bush telegraph remains a mystery to me. A host of questions quickly overpowers one's lamentable knowledge of the neighborhood's ecosystem. And then there's the obsessive drilling of the woodpecker, an elegant bird to be sure, fashioning a hole in the house's timber frame wide enough to accommodate an errant golf ball. On balance I can live with the depredations of deer, chipmunks and woodpeckers; their cuteness secures their pardon. The squadrons of green-bellied fireflies and Hitchcockian jackdaws I can also just about tolerate, but I draw the line when it comes to arachnids (most determinedly in the case of the to-be-avoided-at-all-costs brown recluse or fiddleback, so called because of the violin-shaped mark on the back of its head) or snakes, such as the prime specimen (Northern Copperhead? Black Rat?) that wrapped itself around my horrified, suburb-dwelling secretary's ornamental birdhouse. These creatures should be confined to Indy zoo or the Australian outback, not muscling in on our territory.

Isaiah Berlin, drawing on a line from the Greek poet Archilochus, once characterized dons—it's that word again—as either hedgehogs who know one big thing or foxes who know many things: I confess to being more foxy than prickly. To the best of my knowledge the patrician Berlin never set foot in Bloomington, home to a lobby group—I jest not—known as CLUCK (Citizens Love Urban Chickens), but he certainly seems to have identified intuitively with our rich, feral culture from the comfort of his Oxonian armchair.

Family Affairs

It was the Federal Express Christmas card that got me thinking. Not the card itself, you understand, but the inscription: 'From the FedEx Family.' What family? FedEx is an enormous company operating in a cutthroat market with thousands of employees scattered far and wide. Whatever else it may be, it's certainly not a family. That's taking the notion of a family, even a hyper-extended family, too far. And, anyway, since when did families send typed greetings cards? Just who do the marketing people at FedEx think they are kidding? Presumably, the same people who daily hear the following words from Matt Lauer on the *Today Show*: 'We'll be right back after these messages.' Messages, my foot! What he means is advertisements, but, presumably, the truth is too unpalatable for us to digest that early in the morning along with our bran flakes.

Does printing the words 'FedEx Family' on a bland Christmas card make the recipient feel in any way warm and fuzzy? Do we really imagine that FedEx is, or sees itself as, a family any more than I believe that Indiana University is one big happy family? Of course not, but the early signs of self-delusion are hard to ignore. I've sat in amazement as successive presidents of Indiana University have referred, in both speech and writing, to the IU family. Now, nepotism may have made this an apt metaphor for some small, early modern European universities, but 17th century Basel isn't 21st century Bloomington.

Recently, I received a letter from President Herbert acknowledging some modest accomplishment on my part, but the pleasure was dulled by his writing on 'behalf of the entire Indiana University family,' as if the great majority of my faculty colleagues knew or cared in the slightest. Next a copy of his State of the Union address, which opened: 'Once a year we come together as members of the Indiana University family to reflect...' Well, we don't: at most a few hundred of the many thousand members of this non-existent family come to hear what the sitting president has to say.

The cheery Chancellor of the Indianapolis campus riffed enthusiastically on the family theme in his installation speech: 'I celebrate my own family today, but I also celebrate the IUPUI family.' One should not be surprised. This, after all, is the man who with his scholar-spouse pens Christmas verse for our delectation. Here is a sample: 'Then, out in the news arose such a clatter, / Chancellor Charles leaped to attention, to see what was the matter. / Away to the press conference, he flew like a flash, / Big gifts to two centers had made quite a splash.' Eat yer heart out, Rabbie Burns.

But the Pulitzer for family schmaltz goes to (I'll spare his blushes) an anonymous administrator for this email to the faculty: 'Babies have arrived in our Informatics family as well...In all of this it's easy to get grumpy about something or someone...to be critical or cynical of procedures or each other...Let's take a walk or have a cup of tea together.'

Even the local TV station, WTIU, talks of its 'membership family.' For the record, IU has more than 100,000 faculty, staff and students all told. Add in living alumni, and you're well past the half million mark. A family of that magnitude is hard to imagine, even if you're a rabbit double-dosing on Viagra. As we all know, university departments, to take a more manageable unit of analysis, are, if the family metaphor must be used, a perfect illustration of the...dysfunctional family. Even in the ancient cloisters of Oxbridge, the dons are anything but family-like in their behaviors—just read C.P. Snow's *The Masters*. Compare a modern university with a corporation, a holding company or a large professional practice, if you must, but certainly not with a family.

What lies behind this penchant for the inapt metaphor: 'FedEx Family' for 'hoards of employees,' 'family' for 'sprawling university community'? Why do otherwise intelligent individuals and organizations talk down to us? Why do they debase language; and why does no one seem to care? We see this trend elsewhere, of course, when Pentagon spokespersons refer, euphemistically, to human casualties as 'collateral damage,' and successful air attacks are labeled 'surgical strikes,' as if one were talking about an episode of *ER* rather than bloodshed in Basra. We may not like this pasteurization of the unpalatable, but the logic is easy to grasp and the practice has been exhaustively analyzed by sociolinguists. Geoffrey Nunberg has noted that the language of war is becoming more and more businesslike, with tanks and planes being relabeled 'assets' (business speak, in turn, has long relished military analogies). Sanitized speech has become a depressing norm. Individuals who are handicapped are repackaged as 'alternatively abled,' as if such alliterative re-branding of reality might somehow make one feel better about oneself. Ontological legerdemain is all the rage, in academe and beyond. What would today's incorrigibly PC administrators make of Philip Larkin's quirky observations that holidays are 'an entirely feminine concept,' or that fellow poet Ted Hughes was like 'a Christmas present from Easter Island'?

Again, one has to ask, who's fooling whom? Why the 'IU family?' Why package something that is far removed from most people's definition of a family in such a silly fashion? Family implies blood relations, proximity, tight kinship structures and a shared identity. The answer is simple: since family members presumably look out for one another, members of the globally distributed IU family will look out for their own. And how will they do that? By making gifts and creating endowments to support successive generations. In that respect, IU is, of course, no different from any other institution of higher education in this country; it's just a shame they all resort to the same tired trope to get their eleemosynary messages across.

The Last Supper

Paris has *La Tour d'Argent*, London the Ritz. Bloomington, not to be outdone, had Ladyman's Café, which was about as far removed from *haute cuisine* as *quai de la Tournelle* is from Kirkwood. Still, this was no run-of-the-mill grits, gravy and grease joint: instead, think bacon like grandma made, shimmering sunny side up eggs and golden French fries. On a good day it was hard to beat; on an off day, when chunky white gravy and stodgy biscuits were in the ascendant, it still knocked the socks off much of the local competition. Come Sunday, the menu included the assonance-loaded 'grilled ground round with sautéed onions' and, for Jackson Pollock fans, 'chicken tenders with dripping sauce.' Neither, to my knowledge, can be had at *La Tour d'Argent* or MoMA's Café 2.

Ladyman's had been, in its own words, 'a Bloomington tradition since 1957.' Pancakes and home-baked goodies ('Try a piece of our fabulous pie; better than Robert Redford cake.') will be replaced by an anonymous office block for Finelight Strategic Marketing Communications. As the present owner put it: 'I thought nothing would come through and

change that homey, old-fashioned atmosphere of downtown.' Hadn't
Ms. Reynolds heard of the Wal-Mart effect, was my first thought? My
second was: why couldn't the city fathers see the wisdom of trying
to preserve a slice of historic downtown life? But given that former
Bloomington mayor, John R. Fernandez, was Finelight's senior vice
president for business development, perhaps I was being just as naïve as
the community-spirited Ms. Reynolds. It's one more example of what
has been called 'the yuppification of Bloomington.'

As possibly the only academic dean to show his face regularly in
Ladyman's, I was right behind the rightly aggrieved proprietor and showed
my solidarity by buying the café's hugely popular sweatshirt. Ladyman's
was authentic. It could not have been faked. The décor, even after the
last makeover, left something to be desired. This higgledypiggledy
diner, with its anemic photographs of bygone Bloomington, cheap
fittings and over-exposed entrails, made the cosmopolitan gut heave
before stomach-settling chow was dispatched from the bustling kitchen,
ruled over for 49 years by taciturn chef Jack Covert, whose working day
began at the same time as the average frat boy's Saturday night ended.

Ladyman's won rave reviews over the years and on the Web: 'For
only $5.57 you can walk out full and not feel like crap from all the
alcohol you drank the night before at Nick's Pub.' And bearing out
my amateur observation regarding authenticity: 'This place is the real
deal. No fancy furniture, menus, dishes, waitresses...nuthin...just good
food served reasonably fast.' It was hard to disagree with these citizen
critics.

So, back we all came, sometimes queuing in the sleet to get a
famished toe in the careworn door. In an age of sterile chains, sushi
bars and drive-through restaurants, there was something reassuring
about a family-run eatery that served up comfort food and good cheer.
The genial waitresses, run off their feet, brought Sunday sustenance

and salvation to hung-over undergraduates, salt-of-the-earth Hoosiers, starchily-attired church-goers, down-at-heelers…and me and the kids. Grease brought us together. Class distinctions may not have been erased in this diner of yesteryear, but every so often for a brief spell we were as one.

Despite the sweatshirts, stories in the *Herald-Times* and low-voltage outrage of the regulars, Goliath bested David. The lights went out, the shutters came down and Mr. Covert stayed under the sheets. Ladyman's, the great leveler, will be missed.

Glit Lit

Oscars for actors, Bookers for writers. Prizes, be they Pulitzers or Turners, are an inescapable part of contemporary culture. IU holds its own in the prize stakes: Jazz professor David Baker is an Emmy Award winner; Douglas Hofstadter (as in the 'Hofstadter butterfly') won a Pulitzer (and American Book Award) for *Gödel, Escher, Bach,* and Susan Gubar, co-author (with Sandra Gilbert) of *Madwomen in the Attic*, was a Pulitzer Prize nominee. Ernie Pyle's Pulitzer is from another generation. The conventions and criteria for granting intellectual, artistic and literary awards may vary, but no field of creative endeavor is complete without its very own cabinet of blue ribands and gold medals. The unsung are the *plebs sordida* of our prize-besotted world.

From Tinseltown to the Tate, luvvies and artists are nominated, honors bestowed and statuettes clutched in dizzying succession. The season seems never to end, as awards and ever-increasing largesse are dispensed to grandees, newbies and *enfants terribles* alike. But today's symbolic capital markets are anything but egalitarian in nature. Fame begets fame; the most glittering of the glitterati are quickly on to their second Grammy before most tyros have made their first shortlist: Jack Nicholson has three Oscars and a dozen nominations to his credit, enough to dishearten many a resting thespian. It's not that different in the literary world. Salman Rushdie has not only a slew of coveted awards but also a unique meta prize: a Booker of Bookers. Today, no self-respecting writer's, or professor's, curriculum vitae is complete without a prize or two. Just take a look at IU music professor Menahem Pressler's webpage.

Of course, there are prizes…and prizes. Pride of place goes to the Nobel, first awarded more than a century ago. The citation can be as sparing as the prize is lustrous: 'The Nobel Prize in Literature for 2005 is awarded to the English writer Harold Pinter *who in his plays uncovers the precipice under everyday prattle and forces entry into oppressions' closed rooms.*'' Over the decades, the committee's choices have often provoked controversy: politics and national bias sometimes seeming to trump pure literary merit. Joyce, Proust and Tolstoy didn't make the grade, but Iceland and Guatemala have each secured one, though we might struggle to name those countries' laureates. The Nobel is not exactly a gerontocracy—Kipling was only 42 when the call to Stockholm came—but it does fall squarely into the lifetime achievement category, whether it be for literature, physics or economics.

Indiana University's equivalent of the Nobel is the coveted title of Distinguished Professor, an honor that is bestowed with even greater secrecy and no less backroom politicking than the Gong of All Gongs. Recipients, a brace or so a year, receive a meager annual emolument of approximately $1,500, but, of course, what really matters is being admitted to IU's most exclusive club. Once in, one naturally does one's utmost to keep others out. There's a pecking order in academia, and some of our colleagues have sharp beaks.

The Nobel Prize for literature is currently worth about $1.3 million, enough to abandon the garret in favor of a SoHo loft. No other prize can compete in terms of cash value, but when it comes to pedigree and cachet the Nobel does not exercise an absolute monopoly; most of us would give our right eye for a Pulitzer or the *Prix Goncourt*. However, many awards are little known and topically specific, if not downright quirky: the *Literary Review* Bad Sex in Fiction award was not one that Tom Wolfe seemed to appreciate, feeling that the subtle irony of his prize-winning campus sex scene in *I Am Charlotte Simmons* went over the judges' heads. Me? I would settle gleefully for the Bollinger Everyman Wodehouse Prize for Comic Writing: a case of vintage champagne and (yes) the naming of a pig after the winning novel. But there's the small matter of the novel.

The media's insatiable interest in literary prizes has as much to do with the politics and personalities involved as the literary quality of the works under consideration. At times, the razzamatazz surrounding prize giving relegates authors and their books to the background: the credentials of, and internecine squabbling among, celebrity judges are what seem to matter most. Nonetheless, it would be hard to deny the commercial benefits of being short-listed for, or awarded, a major literary prize: the results register in the publisher's bottom line and the writer's bank balance. Just as an Oscar nomination can boost box office receipts and DVD sales, being nominated for a major prize can propel a book (and its author) out of obscurity onto the bestseller lists. In fact, you won't need a nomination if you can get the Venezuelan president, Hugo Chávez, to endorse your book. After the chubby *caudillo* appeared at the United Nations brandishing a (Spanish language) copy of *Hegemony or Survival*, Professor Chomsky's tome surged to the number one spot on Amazon's bestseller list.

The ante is being raised steadily when it comes to prize money. Bragging rights count in this game, which is good news for both indigent and not so indigent authors. The International IMPAC Dublin Literary Award, self-described as 'the largest and most international prize of its kind,' will hand over $130,000 for a novel written in English and deemed to have 'high literary merit.' It is hardly surprising that Dublin would seek to capitalize on its formidable literary heritage in this fashion, but she does not have it all her own way. Swansea was quick to figure out that a hefty prize named after a literary lion might boost cultural tourism in the area. The £60,000 Swansea Dylan Thomas Prize, launched on the anniversary of the Welshman's birthday (and, yes, the roistering writer visited Bloomington in the spring of 1950 and *may* have had a tipple or two in Nick's), goes to the writer (under 30) of the best book (any genre) in English, published anywhere (in the world). How many more strategic couplings of this kind are in the works, I wonder? Bloomington and...?

I don't know if the inevitable upswing in the sales of short-listed titles typically comes at the expense of other books—a zero sum outcome, if you will—or whether there is a net overall increase in book sales as a result of all the marketing and advertising effort that surrounds literary prize giving. But even if the ballyhoo does not always bump up retail sales or public library lending statistics, quite a few playwrights, professors and poets will be materially better off, either directly (cash prize in hand) or indirectly (future royalty checks), as a result of the media attention.

Predictably, these Caucus-races are attracting the attention of cultural theorists, but much still remains to be said on the changing conditions of literary production and consumption and the long-term effects of these changes on perceptions of literary worth and bookselling trends. Has the culture of prize giving caused publishers to value prize-winning potential more than literary merit? Is the progressive commodification of literature making it harder for new names to break through? I don't know the answers, but I happily confess that my first royalty check for *Bloomington Days* was in the sum of $46.03. Such is the sorry fate of the un-prized. Time to write a best-selling textbook, methinks.

Bag Ladies of Bloomington

They come in two kinds—both the ladies and the bags. There are those pushing a shopping cart stuffed with plastic sacks shrouding life's detritus and those slinging bags convex with chicness and the accoutrements of wealth. The former is likely to be an alcoholic or perhaps a rare tenure case gone sadly awry. By way of an aside, a Minnesota-based insurance company has found that many women have a deep-seated, if irrational, fear of ending their days as a bag lady— 'bag lady syndrome' or 'tramp syndrome' to use the terminology *du jour*. The other kind of bag lady is a 'tanorexic' sorority sister who thinks that ancient Greek is what Pi Beta Phi members got up to at a date party last semester. There are very few, mercifully, of the former in Bloomington, battalions of the latter.

At Indiana University some 5,000 young adults have pledged themselves to the contrived frivolity and conformity that define Greek life; we have 25 active fraternities and 19 active sororities. Fraternity boys, with their baseball caps and reversed heads, open-sided Jeeps and party kegs, give groupthink a bad name—grope-think would be closer to the mark. The cameo appearance by a trio of beer-swigging frat boys in *Borat* merely confirmed one's prejudices. Sorority girls have attracted their fair share of scorn, but they do have a knack of making Britney Spears seem rather smart. If you think Theotokopoulos is a nude beach in Crete rather than that painter guy, El Greco, then, let me assure you, you're candidate material for the ranks. These students with their grating Valspeak are not the bicycling undergraduates of Betjeman's couplet: 'Kant on the handle-bars, Marx in the saddlebag.' But perhaps I shouldn't tar all Greeks with the same brush. Thanks to a $2,400 grant from the Department of Homeland Security, 12 IU fraternity and sorority members are learning lifesavings skills in the event of disaster striking. I, for one, shall sleep more soundly in my bed knowing that Bloomington's preppiest are on stand-by.

In case you haven't noticed, Ugg-booted sorority sisters, when not jamming their fingers down their throats in an effort to achieve 'postwaif' proportions, wear designer sunglasses high on their meticulously streaked hair so that we can better see the letters D&G, as if the initials of two Italian homosexuals mattered one iota. But, even more importantly, these size zeros stuff tweedy Longchamps or Fendi Baguettes over or under their arms so that we know that they know what counts in life. Think Magritte: *ceci n'est pas un sac…* A baguette, for the uninitiated, is a bag in the style of a French loaf—a textbook case of function following form. According to *The New Yorker*, the enterprising Sylvia Fendi has sold some six hundred thousand of these classy containers to status-craving souls around the globe. Baguettes—average cost: $1,500—sell like hot cakes. French loaves, hot cakes: these dough-eyed victims of 'affluenza' may not be able to tell a duffle bag from a Vera Bradley hip hugger after the fourth Tequila Slammer, but they are indefatigable followers of fashion.

Of course I'm guilty of stereotyping, but the antics of a large minority, unfortunately, shape public perceptions. Luxury and looks are what matter for these princesses of privilege. At nearby DePauw University, 23 members of Delta Zeta were evicted recently from their house on spurious grounds; the rejects just happened to include all those who were overweight or non-Caucasian (or both). Members of IU's DZ chapter hastened to Greencastle to help their struggling sisters recruit suitable (i.e., blond, beautiful, size 8) replacements to their depleted ranks. The story graced the pages of the *New York Times* and disgraced the sorority. DePauw's President Bottoms, up to his uxters in damage limitation, finally kicked the chapter off campus.

Sorority sisters rarely walk alone. They emerge in pairs, or packs of five, from their lairs on Third St. or Jordan, pony tails bobbing, bottoms wiggling, cell phones jammed to their ears, side by side but cocooned in their own micro social worlds. The bitchiness and vacuity of these 'friendster whores' have been achingly exposed by Alexandra Robbins in her bestseller, *Pledged*. Ms. Robbins' popularity rating on Greek Row is about that of President Bush's in Sadr City. She could have called her book *Barbie Dolls and Bulimia*, and not been guilty of serious misrepresentation. She didn't, which is probably why she lives to write another day. Robbins bravely gave a public lecture on overachievement at the IU Journalism School this semester and emerged unscathed.

For some light relief I have been flicking through the pages of *Arrow*, the quarterly magazine of Pi Beta Phi (it could just as well have been the quarterly of Phi Mu, Delta Delta Delta or any other sorority) in an attempt to improve my knowledge of this simple-minded sub-culture. Pi Phi, as it likes to be known, doesn't just have a President; it has a Grand President, who signs off her editorial column with the tag 'Ring ching.' I learned that only Grand Presidents can have an obituary published in the magazine, that Pi Phi is indeed a brand (like Coca Cola) in the eyes

of its grandees, that there is a Pi Phi cookbook in the works ('Pi this
in the kitchen,' trills the table of contents), that philanthropy, literacy
and leadership ('We are all leaders') are valued, and that notables in the
Fraternity (that is, after all, how these ladies anachronistically describe
their organization) are reading books with titles such as *The Masters
of Success* and *Life of Pi*. It is hard to take exception to such utterly
unexceptional content; equally, it is hard not to wonder what any of
this has got to do with higher education.

But why take it out on the Greeks? After all, clubs and societies
have been part of university life since time immemorial: Yale has
long had its secretive Skull and Bones society (read *Stover at Yale* for a
glimpse into the arcana of these cabals), Oxford its dashing Bullingdon
Club (satirized as the Bollinger Club in Waugh's *Decline and Fall*),
Cambridge the Apostles (a.k.a. the Cambridge Conversazione Society),
and Heidelberg its dueling clubs and culture of 'bragging scars'. But
for every Pi Beta Phi there is a dozen other Alpha Delta Gammas in
Bloomington. Fraternities and sororities account for 17% of the student
body on campus. If this were true only of IU it would be depressing
enough; that IU is but one of many campuses hosting self-serving social
networks masquerading as scholastically inclined do-gooders is a sorry
reflection on U.S. higher education.

Celebrity Challenged

Celebrity is the undisputed coin of the realm. Today, pedigree, education, aesthetic sensibility and moral authority count for little. Nothing, but nothing, matters more than fame—except perhaps infamy. Being famous for being famous is often as good as it gets. Old money, naturally, knows its place and avoids the media limelight; new money, however, craves attention and pays up-front for the Klieg lights; we live in a 'culture of no culture,' as Nelson Aldrich put it, one in which teenagers consider 'becoming a celebrity' an occupational choice alongside nursing, bookkeeping or plumbing.

The emergence of a celebritocracy is a global phenomenon. *Hola!* magazine and its polyglot derivatives, with more than a little help from the supermarket tabloids, CNN and the Entertainment Channel, provide a range of platforms for 'sublebrities,' *parvenus* and minor royalty to garner a few shekels for cravenly exposing their vacuous lives and complete lack of taste to the gullible masses. Even the BBC has succumbed: 'Does God exit?' invites celebrities ranging from Lucasian Professor of Mathematics, Stephen Hawking, to Dolly Parton (the thinking man's Pamela Anderson) to offer their views on *the* big question.

Once upon a time famous people were great athletes (Jesse Owens), divas (Maria Callas), statesmen (Sir Winston Churchill), or military commanders (Field Marshal Lord Montgomery), a far cry from the likes of the salacious Paris Hilton ('cheaper than a Brooklyn pier hot dog back in 1949, and as sexy as Boy George in drag'—Taki). Psychologists have discovered recently that celebs are different from the likes of you and me: they exhibit extreme levels of self-love and have a compulsive need for public attention. What would we do without psychologists? These days, too, there are 'celebrity pets,' that is to say, pets that are celebrities in their own right. If your collie or cobra has starred in a movie or TV commercial, some airlines will let it travel in the first-class cabin: the mere pet of a celebrity will not, however, be granted such a privilege. This is the realm of non-transferable celebrity.

In the good old days, fame was usually hard won and, whether you liked or disliked the person in question, typically merited. The reigning queen of tackiness is Ms. Hilton, though there is no shortage of credible claimants to the throne. Today's C-list celebrities, most of whom couldn't distinguish a Warhol from a warthog, want only one thing: their fifteen delirious minutes of fame. This, after all, is an age in which news about TV news anchors is deemed as newsworthy as real news. Superficiality has been transmuted into an art form, with spin-doctors earning more than skin doctors. A-list celebrities have become a species apart. 'Civilians,' is how the pouting English movie star, Elizabeth Hurley, refers to those of us who remain firmly beyond the celebrity pale. In her world, and in the words of the society magazine, *Tatler*, there are two castes: the haves and have-yachts. The 'insolence of wealth,' to use Dr. Johnson's phrase, is impossible to ignore.

In an 'economy of attention' the trick is to wrest the spotlight from the other person. As the stakes rise, so does the tawdriness of the tactics employed by career celebrities to hook eyeballs. Insulting George Bush to his face (assuming you can get close enough), flamboyantly entering rehab, or simply dropping one's pants within range of a primed paparazzo are all potentially effective tactics, but the inflationary spiral is such that you may have to gun down another Beatle or garrote a Dutch movie director in broad daylight with a blunt Bowie knife while screaming '*Allah Akhbar!*' to secure your full fifteen minutes of media attention.

The allure of celebrity knows no bounds. Taki, the *Spectator's* unflinching chronicler of the high life, tells of a priest at a baptism signaling to the officiating cardinal to inch closer to supermodel Elle Macpherson so that a snap can be taken. Apparently, God's scarlet-socked men can't resist 'skinny bones'. Even academia, for all its high-mindedness, is not immune to the siren call of celebrity, though we are less inclined to pimp our rides in the manner of rap's aristocracy—a Toyota Prius metamorphosing into a Toyota Priapus in the IU Library parking lot is hard to imagine.

We fuddy-duddies do have a splattering of *galácticos* in our midst: think, for example, of the colorful Stanley Fish—once described by Terry Eagleton as 'the Donald Trump of American academia'—who helped put Duke on the map; or the pugnacious Camille Paglia, who has knocked more noses out of joint than Mike Tyson; or the high-minded Cornel West, who hip-hopped from Harvard to Princeton; or the late Edward Saïd of Columbia, who was involved in a high-profile, rock-chucking escapade on the Lebanon-Israel border. Visibility is not, of course, synonymous with creativity or integrity, but for every Ward Churchill in our hallowed groves there is, mercifully, a soft-spoken Roger Kornberg, a Nobel laureate, whose talents and accomplishments, regrettably, may not always attract quite as many column inches as the posturing prof. One should be careful not to confuse media visibility with originality of thought, though on rare occasions the two are coextensive, as in the case of MIT's Noam Chomsky.

Indiana University—the Jacobs School of Music apart—is, it has to be said, somewhat celebrity challenged. It's not that we lack brilliant brains, it's just that brilliance is taken for granted in our community of minds: it's the base line in this line of work. It's no secret that IU has no current Nobel laureates of which to boast, nor anyone with the public visibility of, say, Harvard's Alan Dershowitz or Oxford's Richard Dawkins, at least not since the demise of the remarkable Alfred Kinsey. (The cinquain below, whimsically inserted here I concede, is by my good friend and late-life versifier, Michael Davenport.)

Kinsey
He had
the gall to move
from wasp taxonomies
to study sex among the guys
and gals.

These days, celebrity is more likely to be acquired through association or by happenstance. When cyclist Lance Armstrong was diagnosed with testicular cancer in the mid-nineties, he sought the pioneering treatment developed by Dr. Lawrence H. Einhorn, a clinical oncologist at the Indiana University Cancer Center. The seven-time *Tour de France* winner's recovery made Einhorn—a Distinguished Professor at IU and a nationally recognized expert in his field—something of a celebrity. Along with considerable peer esteem, Dr.

Einhorn now has some mainstream media magnetism, having saved Armstrong's manhood.

Speaking of image brings us to another contemporary celebrity: Jared Fogel. When a student at Bloomington, Mr. Fogel weighed a whopping 425 lbs. This hard-to-miss fact shaped his curricular choices (these, sadly, were the days before Fat Studies) in that he had to be sure that the classes he planned to take were scheduled in auditoria fitted with sufficiently capacious seats. To cut a long and not terribly interesting story short, Jared—whose physique was strikingly different from that possessed by another famous IU alumnus, the sculpted, seven-time Olympic gold medal swimmer, Mark Spitz—stumbled upon Subway and soon thereafter Subway stumbled upon a slimmed down Jared who subsequently starred in a series of TV commercials for the sandwich chain, while landing both an appearance on Oprah and the inevitable book deal. According to the *Herald-Times*, Jared is 'recognized everywhere he goes, from Australia to Orlando to Seattle…' which, I suspect, is more than can be said for almost every professor at IU.

I have never met either the beefed up or slimmed down Jared. I did, however, once speak briefly to Noam Chomsky when he gave a talk in our department and I almost got a word in edgeways. I chatted amiably to the *émigré* conductor Raymond Leppard, then at the helm of the Indianapolis Symphony, as we waited for the commencement procession to begin; he was to receive an honorary doctorate. I clasped Umberto Eco's hand at a university dinner, but before I could launch an opening inanity both he and his well-versed hand were gone. William Merwin, sometime poet laureate, couldn't withdraw so easily; I was his designated driver for the night. I don't know if any of these four gentlemen is, or would ever wish to be considered, a celebrity of sorts, but each of them has done immeasurably more for mankind than Jared

Fogel and Paris Hilton combined could ever hope to accomplish. But the aforementioned Mr. Fattypuff and Miss Thinifer, along with the designer-labeled ranks of the WAGS (Wives And GirlfiendS...of the England football players), are what pass for celebrity these days. *Sic transit gloria mundi,* as Rosie O'Donnell would say.

In Full Bloom

'Leopold Bloom ate with relish the inner organs of beasts and fowl.' With these words James Joyce introduces the reader of *Ulysses* to one of literature's best-known characters. The fictional Bloom had a son, Rudy, and the equally fictional Mrs. Bloom had an affair with her manager, one Blazes Boylan. Begosh and begorrah! Now, is my name not Blaise, do I not hold a Rudy professorship and do I not myself hail from the land of Anna Livia? And was Saint James not born in 41 Brighton Square and do I not have a bolt-hole in Brighton of all places? And is *Bloom* not the name of the magazine right now before my very own eyes and is that magazine not all about life in Bloomington, my adopted hometown? And, furthermore, is not *Rudy* also the name of a movie, whose screenwriter, Angelo Pizzo, son of an alumna of my school, is both an interviewer for, and interviewee in, *Bloom*? The filaments of coincidence are at once so teasingly revealed, so compellingly entwined. Let us all rejoyce!

Bloom is a real magazine; no advertorials, no puff. It can hold its own with the best of breed. It's airily designed and professionally

produced and I'm pleased to report that its regular columnists can
distinguish between a verb and a noun. I have just read the first
three bi-monthly issues back-to-back. The city reflected in these
pages is an island of understated charm, culture and creativity. Is
this really *my* Bloomington? Our Cinderella city has rarely presented
so well. If I didn't live here, I'd relocate without a second thought,
which is precisely what Malcolm Abrams did, abandoning a magazine
publishing career in NYC to put down mid-life roots in B-town and
launch *Bloom*. And, yet, something was missing. The quirkiness
of the place seems to have ceded to gloss. The warts and all were
nowhere to be seen. In the world of commercial publishing, warts, of
course, may not have a place. Local businesses generate the advertising
revenue that keeps the magazine afloat, so, for instance, pointing out
that retail therapy is well nigh impossible in Bloomington might not
be an astute move.

Familiarity and credibility are essential ingredients. We must be able
to recognize ourselves and the city portrayed in the magazine. Along
with resonance we also expect to be taken to an elevated appreciation
of our *milieu*, what I'll call the 'I had no idea' factor. *Bloom* achieves
a good balance between reassuring familiarity and pleasant surprise,
my warts-related reservations notwithstanding. But I need not descant
on it further; decide for yourself.

Pat Baude writes the 'Wining' column. He is no shrinking violet
('The texture is close to creamy, surprising in a wine with such an airy
profile.') but he's also no Jancis Robinson, M.W.: 'quintessentially an
aperitif, but if you were to drink it with a well-dressed salad, it would
not rise up to bite you.' Mr. Baude showed up in my office some
months ago, but at that time I was interacting with a constitutional
law professor not someone whose Paul of Tarsus moment came at
the age of sixteen when granted a small glass of Château Margaux as

a birthday treat. Had I but known. Ah, how the conversation might have meandered in other directions, as I did that day, many years ago, when, gawping at Madame Mentzelopoulos's neoclassical pile, the urge to relive myself in less than imperial style suddenly proved irresistible.

For those who like slow food, another co-opted academic, Christine Barbour, writes spryly about world cuisine, turkey types and local produce, but she has yet to educate us on the inner organs of beasts and fowl, so relished by the cuckolded Mr. Bloom. Completing the donnish trio of regular columnists is Master Gardener—that's a title, not a casual encomium—Moya Andrews, who is as comfortable on paper as she is on the local airwaves describing horticultural tricks of the trade for green-fingered residents of south central Indiana.

Should jazz be your thing, Bloomington is only one sandwich short of a New Orleans picnic. It helps, of course, to have a music school with a stonker of a jazz program, created by the estimable David Baker. Gifted teachers and students naturally need outlets for their talents, and Bloomington has a wide variety of jazz haunts, from the colorful *Cafe Django* (owned and operated by the Dalai Lama's brother and sister-in-law) and the spatially endowed *tutto bene* to the gritty granddaddy of them all, *Bear's Place*, in which talents, traditional and postmodern, can be showcased and enjoyed. Living here, you won't need a CD collection.

Fashion and furnishings, antiques and eateries, sport and the performing arts, *Bloom* has its target down to a tee, but just manages to avoid, if I may appropriate Richard Halpern's words, 'Norman Rockwell's manufactured innocence.' Will the advertising dollars continue to flow in? Can a solid subscriber base be established in such a small community? Is there sufficient life post-Lotus Festival to sustain the gloss? I don't know the answers to these questions, but I certainly hope they incline to the affirmative. In Dublin, Bloomsday is celebrated every June 16th, but here we can now celebrate the occasion half a dozen times a year. 'Six bloomin' good glasses of burgundy and six Gorgonzola sandwiches that'll be, barman.'

Ghost Writing

The phrase 'ghost in the machine' was coined by Gilbert Ryle in 1949. The British philosopher used it originally in *The Concept of Mind*, a spirited attack on Cartesian dualism—'the Dogma of the Ghost in the Machine,' to be precise. Many have since appropriated Ryle's clever coinage. Arthur Koestler, one of the great polymaths of our time, published his book, *The Ghost in the Machine,* in my freshman year. It takes issue with B.F. Skinner and behaviorism. Skinner, by the way, was for nine years a faculty member in IU's Department of Psychology before decamping to Harvard. He wrote his classic paper, '"Superstition" in the pigeon' while here. Why only the pigeon?

I mention all of this because of one word: ghost. In academia it's fine to discuss metaphorical ghosts (in seminars on literary criticism, philosophy of mind, or artificial intelligence) but not the other kind—unless you want to put your career at risk. Research into the paranormal is not the surest route to tenure or peer acclaim, yet a few bold souls have deemed the risk worth taking. Edinburgh University has a small parapsychology unit, funded from Koestler's estate, which is committed to 'the scientific study of the capacity attributed to some individuals to interact with their environment by means other than the recognised sensorimotor channels.' I don't know how you could persuade me that you've seen a ghost, but by the same token I know I can't know that ghosts don't exist. I guess that leaves me somewhere between Karl Popper and Donald Rumsfeld in the epistemology stakes.

Halloween routinely brings out our barely contained craving to believe in the paranormal. Even the *Financial Times* couldn't resist the temptation to get in on the act; its holiday *House & Home* section assessed the effect of a haunting on property values. The article was not a wayward April Fool's piece but a sober assessment of the economic costs of *en suite* spooks. As Samuel Johnson remarked apropos the subject: 'All argument is against it, but all belief is for it.'

Universities have more than their fair share of ghosts and ghouls: *Haunted Halls of Ivy* is devoted exclusively to spooky Southern colleges and universities. This paranormal malarkey is really quite normal, it would seem. In fact, when I first visited Bloomington I was taken to dinner in Portico's restaurant, where my hosts told me that the sounds of children laughing and playing upstairs could often be heard, even though there were no children. I heard nothing that night, though I strained throughout the insipid dinner table conversation to hear what I really wanted to hear. Portico's is now a law office and the children have apparently chosen to be neither seen nor heard since the change.

What's good enough for the *FT* is good enough for IU. A Bloomington campus tradition is the annual 'ghost walk' sponsored by the Department of Folklore and Ethnomusicology. It's all storytelling and harmless, costumed fun, a ramble around several of the allegedly haunted spots on campus. A copywriter on the staff of *IU Home Pages* entitled her piece 'Boo U.' But for some this is no laughing matter. According to the author of *Most Haunted Hoosier Trails*, IU is among the most 'spirited' universities in the nation. Be that as it may, I have yet to be freaked.

Grub around, as I discovered, and the stories soon come tumbling out of the woodwork. Here's a sample, ranging from the comic to the chilling. There's a little boy who mischievously rearranges the silverware on the tables of the Tudor Room in the IMU. Read Hall is haunted by the ghost of a young woman, Paula, who committed suicide in the dorm and also by the ghost of an undergraduate who was stabbed to death by her medical student boyfriend. The university's Career Center is haunted by the spirits of unborn children, a doctor having carried out illegal abortions there. The 11th floor of the Main Library is haunted, and the Lilly Library, too. The ghost of a girl in a yellow nightdress has appeared in one of the underground utility tunnels. And so it goes.

Ghosts are a cross-cultural phenomenon, long part of human history. Timothy Long, a classics professor at IU, has lectured on the subject of Greek and Roman ghost stories. There may be nothing new under the spectral sun, but for those with a yearning to connect with the Other Side, Indiana University may be as good a place as any to start. And, you'll not be alone. The Indiana Ghost Trackers (Bloomington Chapter) are at hand, physically and virtually (via their helpful website), to provide training, advice and encouragement to those interested in the paranormal and ghost hunting. I doubt, though, that you'll encounter many members of IU's (lately renamed) Department of Psychological and Brain Sciences in their midst. Given the pace of recent advances in cognitive neuroscience, it may not be all that long before ghosts are explained away in terms of the complex workings (or malfunctions) of the brain— epiphenomenal trivia. Spooks may turn out to be a simple case of matter over mind. Or not.

Buck's Fizz

Last time I knocked back a Buck's Fizz (Champagne, orange juice & grenadine syrup) was in the Café Royal, one of Oscar Wilde's favorite haunts. We were celebrating something or other over a leisurely Sunday brunch, dinner at that time being beyond our means. The Café Royal, whose legendary wine cellars lie unsuspected beneath London's magnificent if congested Regent Street, is unabashed Edwardian opulence: gleaming mirrors, sparkling gilt and bordello red. Sir William Orpen's painting, *Café Royal, London, 1912,* captures the spirit of the place—as was. But that is neither here nor there. This vignette is about the big bucks of academe, the bucks that pay for Buck's Fizz and the other luxuries that have become the surreptitious staples of professorial life.

America has more than a few individuals whose net worth could challenge the GDP of some sub-Saharan African nations, and yet only 1% of the U.S. population earns more than $100,000. The disparities in income distribution (84% of wealth is controlled by 12% of the population) may not be on a par with those of Brazil or Mexico, but the concentration of riches is nonetheless breathtaking for a country blessed with such wealth-generating capacity.

What holds at the macro level also holds at the micro level. Bloomington is a small city of modest means with a few well-heeled citizens and Indiana University a public institution of considerable if unexceptional wealth, one that still pays its faculty less than most other Big-10 universities. With the exception of some sorority girls, ostentation is not the done thing in these parts; the cunning ones go for the bumper sticker that says 'My car is a status symbol. It symbolizes my poverty.' To be sure, there are houses of speech crippling vulgarity with seven figure price tags and owners to match—*H&L* (*Homes & Lifestyles of South-Central Indiana*) magazine makes this fact depressingly clear—but in the main Townies and Gownies have managed to avoid the worst forms of conspicuous consumption without the imposition of sumptuary laws. I like to think that the blustery B-school professor who opined that nothing exceeds like excess was speaking tongue-in-cheek; the fearless Oriana Fallaci would likely have characterized the aside as being indicative of America's 'childish cult of opulence.'

Each summer when the *Herald-Times* publishes its list of IU salaries, there is the predictable inhalation of community breath and unbridled anger in some quarters. No fewer than 600 employees were paid $100,000 or more in 2006, of whom 47 earned at least $200,000. However, some 430 individuals made less than $25,000. Said the president of Local 4730 of the Communications Workers of America (CWA): 'If IU could find a way to cut out just a few high-priced administrators and redistribute that money to staff salaries, they could make great strides in providing decent pay and wage equity for all IU employees.' I am only surprised he didn't suggest reallocating the base salaries of both the basketball coach and the football coach; that would generate an additional $1,750 for each CWA employee in the lowest pay bracket according to my back-of-the-envelope reckoning—just enough for a couple of pairs of Manolo Blahnik alligator pumps. Both coaches would still earn a hefty six-figure income from their various media and endorsement contracts, so it would be a win-win outcome, from an equity point of view. And while I'm on the subject of non-academic pay, I wonder what the CWA thinks of the contract extension (2007-2013) awarded to IU's Director of Athletics: an annual salary of $300,000, with $60,000 in deferred compensation, to say nothing of performance-related incentives.

In fairness, I should reiterate that IU is unremarkable in terms of its remuneration policies and practices when it comes to both academics and athletics. Our president's total annual university compensation for fiscal 2006-07 was a relatively modest $465,560 (though he also negotiated a 10-year post-retirement deal which will net him a further $300,000) compared with the $880,950 earned by his opposite number at Purdue. On the sporting front, one third of big-time college coaches pull down more than $1 million; the University of Texas at Austin pays its head football coach a massive $2.55 million. If that's not bad enough, its head basketball coach received a $40,000 bonus because the GPA of his team exceeded 2.45, which, by the way, is pretty close to a C+... and, remember, C+ = 'unsatisfactory work.' Imagine if professors received a cash bonus every time their students produced marginal work, as these plutocrats of play do; imagine if they received $30,000 a year for ten years following their official retirement for doing next to nothing.

The details of the University's contract with the as yet unproven Mr. Sampson have been made available online thanks to the transparency-conscious *IDS*. Over seven years Coach Sampson (who had been found guilty of violating NCAA rules while at Oklahoma—now there's a role model for IU students and staff) will earn $10.8 million, with his first year salary of $1.1 million rising to $1.61 million by July 2007. The university will allocate Sampson two vehicles for use at his personal discretion (I, the longest serving academic dean on campus, don't receive so much as a bicycle for my discretionary use) and a budget of $375,000 for three assistant coaches. Should Coach actually do what he's being paid to do in the first place, namely, win a national championship, he will earn an additional $100,000. (Here is a taste of his post-game analysis: 'Rod threw up a couple of vomit shots the other day.') Showing up would seem to be sufficient to justify paying our lionized coaches their bloated salaries.

Whatever way you look at it, that's an awful lot of Buck's Fizz. But I'll leave the last word to Orson Wells: 'Living in the lap of luxury isn't bad, except that you never know when it is going to stand up.'

Eight Front Doors

I interviewed here in 1990. 'What are your views on the off-campus program, Dr. Cronin?' was the very first question from the search committee. My reply was memorably, though not suicidally, brief: 'What off-campus program?' I had come to Bloomington not knowing that Indiana University operated on eight campuses and that several professional schools had a distributed presence, including the one for which I harbored aspirations to be dean. Despite my woeful ignorance, I got the job; and, *mirabile dictu*, have managed to hang on to it since then. But if I knew then what I know now, I am not sure that I would have accepted the position. By the same token, IU might not have offered me the position.

On my travels over the years I had met several scholars who had spent time at IU, and for them as for me IU was synonymous with Bloomington; regional campuses such as South Bend and New Albany might as well have been on Mars, for all we knew or cared. I, as others, came to Indiana because of Bloomington's academic reputation; Bloomington might not be Berkeley, but for someone from Margaret

Thatcher's Britain this was a place where cherished academic values continued to flourish in a way that was no longer possible in the bean-counting culture promoted by the Iron Lady. But IU was more than Bloomington, I soon discovered.

The remarkable Herman B Wells strove to make higher education accessible to the average Hoosier, and since not all Hoosiers would or could study at Bloomington, he envisaged a network of regional campuses so that no citizen of the state of Indiana would be more than 50 miles from a point of presence. Wells's goal of bringing Townies and Gownies closer together was laudable, but the organizational octopus which he helped create has long since become dysfunctional—though no ranking administrator in his or her right mind would dare stand up and say as much out loud.

Each new IU president struggles from day one to manage a gaggle of irreconcilable institutional egos and ambitions. The smaller regional campuses (community colleges by any other name) have dreams beyond their station while that most bewildering of organizational hybrids IUPUI (Indiana University-Purdue University at Indianapolis) sometimes seems to confuse aspiration with actuality. Not even Solomon could sort out the prolix politics and tortuous history of the Indiana University system.

Thomas Ehrlich came up with the egalitarian 'One University with Eight Front Doors.' His tag line was quickly derided, though that may have been in part because of his penchant for wearing bowties, an unnatural act in the eyes of most locals. His presidential successor, Myles Brand, quickly disassociated himself from the portal metaphor and spoke instead of 'the constellation that is IU.' Early in Brand's tenure, some colleagues at IUPUI took exception when he had the temerity to describe Bloomington as the flagship campus. They gave him a T-shirt with the legend: 'If Bloomington is the flagship, then IUPUI is the starship.' Touché!

I have spent more time than I care to think in featureless Indianapolis over the last sixteen years, interacting with faculty and administrators on that campus. It has not always been an unreservedly enriching experience, and for every soft-spoken Gerald Bepko, an immensely likeable lawyer and sometime IUPUI chancellor who knows his way around the Old Course at St. Andrews as well as he does the bunkers and fairways of Indiana University, there is a brace of week-end duffers. From the very beginning I was struck by the overt hostility towards all things Bloomington. Refer casually to Bloomington as the principal or flagship campus, and the locals became apoplectic. It's what the *IDS* calls the 'IUPUI - whine.' Yet, the truth is simple; if Lord Nelson (forgive the anachronism) were president of IU, his flagship would be named HMS Bloomington.

The statistical evidence is unambiguous; one need only turn to *US News & World Report's* annual survey to see the disparity in academic quality between the two (core, as they are known) campuses. Alternatively, compare the SAT scores of incoming students or year-on-year retention rates on the Bloomington and Indianapolis campuses; the difference is dramatic and probably unbridgeable. But in fairness that is only to be expected. The U.S. higher education system is highly stratified and the rankings, regularly updated and occasionally fine-tuned, are visible to all who care to look. However, some of our IUPUI colleagues prefer to ignore the statistical evidence and stick their heads in the sand.

In his 1996 State of the University address, President Brand described Bloomington as 'a distant descendant of Plato's Academy, Aristotle's Lyceum and, more recently, the German research university founded in the early nineteenth century by great scholars like Wilhelm von Humboldt.' And that, without wishing to sound pretentious, is why most of us are here today and not in Fort Wayne or Gary—no disrespect intended.

The Platonic ties of which Brand spoke are less evident at IUPUI, which is only to be expected, given that it was 'born in 1969.' IUPUI is a different kind of institution, with a markedly different ethos. This snippet from the current chancellor's installation address conveys a sense of what I mean: 'My wife, Sandra Petronio, is on stage today. A preeminent communication scholar, Sandra is my closest faculty colleague, my wisest friend, and my love—Sandra you have given me so much—thank you— Thank you.' Touching and sincere, to be sure, but more Oprah than Plato or Humboldt.

Both individually and in concert, IUPUI and the six regional campuses make undeniably valuable contributions to the state by reaching out to their local communities, but that role is inherently different from the role played by the Bloomington campus, a *refugium* of world-class scholarship and research. Being different is not the same as being bad. But for some that simple message is difficult to digest.

Beckett & Bollocks

What I know about Samuel Beckett could fit on the back of a postage stamp (well, one from San Marino). We both grew up in Ireland, he of Anglo-Irish stock, I a fusion of Anglo-Irish and Celtic bloodlines. Half a century apart, we both read French at Trinity College Dublin. He performed exceptionally well, I unexceptionally. We both visited the National Gallery of Ireland on and off over the years. There, the forced similarities end. He moved to Paris and became a literary icon; I moved to Bloomington and became a con artist.

In either 1967 or 1968 I attended a Trinity Players' production of *Waiting for Godot.* In those days, the little university theater seated 40; it was an intimate and initially perplexing experience. This wasn't Molière, by a long chalk. I didn't quite know how to respond, but I was smart enough to know how not to respond. Then things improved on the Beckett front; I read *More Pricks Than Kicks* and laughed out loud—largely, I confess, from relief. Beckett *was* accessible, sometimes. The same holds true for people who write about Beckett and one or two of those accessible scholars can be found at Indiana University. Other universities seem less fortunate. But I am getting ahead of myself.

I've just been reading *Samuel Beckett: A Passion for Paintings*, a compilation of essays discussing Beckett's lifelong interest in, and knowledge of, art. I learned that *Waiting for Godot* had been inspired, in part, by a small painting ('Two men contemplating the moon') by Caspar David Friedrich—someone for whom I've had a soft spot since first encountering him on the walls of the Ulster Museum in Belfast during my graduate student days. By the way, Beckett and I are in sparkling company; the vampish Camille Paglia has a Friedrich picture ranked #5 on her 'Top Ten Favorite Paintings.'

There's also some interesting information about Beckett's friendship with the painter Jack B. Yeats, currently Ireland's hottest saleroom name and subject of a fine biography by Bruce Arnold. A pair of paintings by Yeats, *Two Travellers* and *The Graveyard Wall*, may also have inspired *En Attendant Godot*. By way of an aside, J.B.'s brother, the Nobel laureate, W.B. Yeats, lectured at IU in the winter of 1904, having first visited Purdue and then Notre Dame, where (I'm reliably informed by Donald Gray, Culbertson Professor Emeritus of English at IU) he found 'the big merry priests...all Irish and proud as Lucifer of their success in getting Jews and non-conformists to their college.'

Things were going well until I came up against a couple of essays by American academics. How do you know you've encountered bollocks? A sure sign is the appearance of the word 'contested' in the opening paragraphs. And so it was with Messrs Allen and Lloyd. Naturally, things got worse, though by no means as bad as they might have. Here's just one example of constipated writing: 'If these works are, as they are, representations of those who "cannot represent themselves" and therefore "must be represented", they are no less representations of that which eludes representation, which disappears from representation even in the glare of what it renders visible.' Quite so, Mr. Lloyd!

You can see why Beckett had little time for critics and academic theorists. Compare this kind of career-boosting prolixity with Beckett's economy of language (and I apologize to the poet William Merwin if I'm distorting his words in the retelling of this dinner table anecdote). At a reception hosted by the British embassy in Paris, a Frenchman says to Beckett: '*Vous êtes anglais, monsieur?*' '*Au contraire,*' replies Beckett. Beckett, you'll note, didn't bang on about the importance of 'a crypto-feminist subaltern perspective' or anything of that sort. Brevity and wit; two words, three syllables. As far as I can tell, Beckett seems to have had an innate antipathy to bollocks of any kind.

Find me a critical theorist who can craft an article that is not padded with words like 'privileging,' 'hegemony,' 'problematized,' 'intertextuality,' 'simulacra,' 'ethnicized,' or who does not prostrate himself at the altar of French pseudo-philosophy, and I'll buy you the complete works of Lacan or Deleuze—in translation, *bien sûr*. It is all too easy to sneer and sneering will be dismissed airily by the ruling élites and their epigones in literary studies departments, but the stylistic contortions and promiscuous speculations of postmodern theorists invite lampoonery, if not the sack. As the novelist Martin Amis noted with admirable English understatement: 'Academic preferment will not come from a respectful study of Wordsworth's poetics; it will come from a challenging study of his politics—his attitude to the poor, say, or his unconscious "valorization" of Napoleon.'

And it's not just in departments of literature and cultural studies that the rot has set in; language abuse is ubiquitous. I found this gem by an associate professor in our School of Education, though perhaps it's another Sokal hoax and I've swallowed it hook, line and sinker. It was on the 'philosophy' section of his webpage, so I infer that it is there to be read and, presumably, taken seriously. Take a deep breath:

'Over the years parents, educators, friends, colleagues, and, eventually, our own selves continually tell us "no," and we learn to oppress, deny, and bury our egos and sense of self. We conform to societal norms without an appreciation for how they align with our personal desires. Passion and individuality are not celebrated and encouraged; rather they are tempered and eventually atrophy...My task as an educator, friend, colleague, and fellow human being is not to "tell" or "socialize" others into some shared perspective, but rather to foster a passion for unique passions. Clearly, I do engage in didactic lectures or even lapse into pedantic instants. However, these pedagogical periods are couched within the context of a larger goal. In other words, they are not ends onto themselves but serve as tools to assist in the attainment of some larger goal to which the students are engaged.'

I immediately thought of this proverb from Mali: 'Slowly but surely the excrement of foreign poets will come to your village.' Our nameless colleague's 'passion' seems to come at the expense of pellucidity. Beckett referred enigmatically to his own work as 'a stain upon the silence;' what, I wonder, would he make of this grotesque textual blemish...and could our beloved Kinser Cleaners, which almost went the way of Ladyman's, rise to the challenge?

Going, Going, Gong

Dame Edith Sitwell was nothing if not blunt. 'Fools,' she once wrote to John Gielgud, 'are made doctors by other fools in other universities, but no fool has ever been given an Hon. D.Litt. by Oxford.' No fool she; her Oxonian gong was awarded in 1951, an occasion which she proclaimed to be 'the proudest and happiest moment of my life.'

Oxford has been conferring honorary doctorates for more than 500 years. The poet John Skelton was granted his honorific by Cambridge in 1493, the first on record for the upstart in the Fens. Since then, many distinguished names have wended their way to the twin towers of British higher education to receive what Mark Twain, himself honored by Oxford, called these 'unearned finds'—of which, by the way, he had a respectable clutch. Twain took the invitation from the city of dreaming spires seriously, crossing the Atlantic to receive his D.Litt. in person.

I don't expect to hear from Oxbridge, but I was tickled pink when Queen Margaret College, Edinburgh, came up trumps. I shan't readily forget the black-tie dinner in the stately home of Lord and Lady Elgin and the pre-prandial Champagne in the withdrawing room, on the walls of which hung fragments of the Elgin marbles. Or the ceremony next day in the baroque splendor of Edinburgh's domed Usher Hall. The other honorees were the Regius Professor of Surgery at Edinburgh University, the jovial CEO of a Scottish software company and the delightful Michelin-starred Prue Leith, who had already acquired half a dozen honorary doctorates for her contributions to the culinary arts and society-at-large. An eclectic bunch, very much par for the course these days.

Commencement and other academic rituals were exported from the Mother Country to the Colonies, and Harvard was the first American college to award an honorary doctorate, to its sitting president in 1692. Yale followed suit in 1723. Later New Haven notables include John F. Kennedy, who remarked famously: 'Now I have the best of all possible worlds, a Yale degree and a Harvard education.'

Come late spring, swarms of kings and commoners, not to mention a confederacy of ex-presidents, from Clinton to Gorbachev, converge on our nation's campuses. Resplendent in their newly-acquired medieval attire, they process with measured gravity through quadrangles and across trim lawns before finally moving center stage for their moment of academic glory. The *dramatis personae* take their places. Brief citations are read. Most often the honorand is mute, a motionless peacock, who has only to doff cap, don hood and clasp parchment before stepping back to make room for the next worthy.

Nobility is always a safe bet at such occasions, be it King Harald of Norway or the Prince of Wales (15 to date). Luminaries such as Nelson Mandela will be surefire successes, though the competition to secure their presence can be fierce. The A-list is short; for every Mandela there are dozens of Don ('American Pie') McLeans, Jane Pauleys or Wayne Gretzkys only too willing to be hooded. Does anyone seriously imagine that these individuals would ever be honored in like fashion by either

Harvard or Oxford? I was a member of the platform party when Pauley, an IU alumna, received her gong—one up, I suppose, from swinging Al Cobine or John Mellencamp, local-boys-made-good. But IU does get it right on occasion; notables during my tenure have included Umberto Eco and Joseph Stiglitz.

Potential donors and corporate leaders are routinely recipients of honorary doctorates (IU cunningly conferred degrees on both local billionaire William Cook and his wife). Some CEOs appear at commencement ceremonies almost as often as they do on the cover of *Fortune* or *Business Week*. Of course, corporations are also frequent donors and some donors have expectations (*Timeo Danaos et dona ferentes*). When McGill University in Canada conferred a doctorate on scientist *cum* entrepreneur, Dr. Richard Tomlinson, it was in return for a $64 million gift to his alma mater: 'We're not going to pretend that it's for anything else. This is our way of saying "thank you",' stated Principal Bernard Shapiro, unapologetically.

Honorary doctorates, like Nobel Prizes, are often bestowed on graying eminences—I am (still) an exception on both counts. These coveted garlands are typically reserved for outstanding lifetime accomplishments. They are certainly not the preserve of young turks. Of course, exceptions can be found. The classical pianist, André Watts—a Yale honoree and currently a faculty member in the Jacobs School of Music—is, I believe, the youngest recipient of an honorary doctorate on record.

The exalted world of the honorary doctorate provides a telling illustration of the Matthew effect: 'For unto every one that hath shall be given, and he shall have abundance.' General 'Black Jack' Pershing received a dozen in a three year period from both British and American universities, a particularly fecund spell by any standard, and all the more impressive when one considers that the conferring institutions included Oxford, Cambridge, Harvard and Yale. Not just quantity, but quality. To date, the playwriting ex-Czech president, Václav Havel, has accumulated about 40, not bad for a central European statesman. The late Herman B Wells garnered 26. The record holder, however, is the Hoosier state's Reverend Theodore M. Hesburgh, President Emeritus of the University of Notre Dame, with 150 gongs.

On the one hand we have scholars of distinction, statesmen, and notables from the fine and performing arts (Francis Crick, Mary Robinson, David Hockney). On the other hand we have a motley crew drawn from the worlds of popular music, sport, and enterprise culture (Gloria Estefan, Jack Nicklaus, Bill Gates). By all means, let our universities continue to bestow the traditional honorary degrees (Litt.D, Sc.D., D.Mus., etc.) on the A-list as appropriate, but—as I proposed, unsuccessfully, to the Trustees of Indiana University a few years ago—for the others it may be time to institute a new kind of honorary doctorate (D.Hon., has been suggested) which is reserved for non-scholarly accomplishments.

That way the pop stars, corporate titans and sporting gods will still have their day in the sun (and the universities their gifts and media moments), but the integrity of the traditional degree—academia's highest honor, when all is said and done—will have been preserved. Dame Edith, one imagines, would approve. I can't, of course, speak for Mr. Mellencamp.

Hostile Climate

Thanks to farsighted President Wells, Thomas Hart Benton's celebrated murals finally came to rest in Bloomington. They had been commissioned for the Indiana Hall at the 1932 Chicago World's Fair. Not everyone was, or is, enamored of Benton's pictorial style or choice of subject matter, though University Chancellor Ken Gros Louis has judiciously described the murals as being as 'inspiring as any Old Master work, yet as down to earth and colloquial as a conversation on the courthouse square.' One mural in particular, *Parks, the Circus, the Klan, the Press*, has had a checkered life since its unveiling in the Hoosier state back in the thirties.

The problem for some is that this mural (Cultural Panel 10), located in a quite splendid Woodburn Hall lecture theater, includes a depiction of the Ku Klux Klan. Over the years, controversy has flared up spasmodically among sections of the black student body, who maintain that the KKK imagery constitutes, in the phraseology of the moment, a 'hostile climate.' The complainants, needless to say, seem not to have noticed or attended to the fact that the work also depicts a white nurse at the bedside of a black child ('little Jiminy and her blonde nurse'). In Indiana, as in life, there are good folks and bad folks. Benton's work tells it like it is. Some blinkered souls don't see it as it is.

In 2002, a group of students called yet again for the offending mural's removal. After much public debate and ostensibly heart-felt discussion across campus, the then chancellor came to a decision: the mural would stay in place but a diversity education program would be built around Benton's offending work. She was absolutely right to say that moving or covering the mural would be 'morally wrong' but undermined her own high moral ground by recasting the central issue as 'the status of diversity on campus.' To make matters worse she announced that 'we need to create...more diverse art, on the Bloomington campus...that will celebrate, recognize and memorialize the multicultural past and present...' Not so: our goal as an institution of learning and a site of cultural reproduction should be to encourage the creation, collection and curation of the best art. Tokenism has no place in the Louvre or Prado, the Fogg or Fitzwilliam; it should have no place here.

Educational sessions now follow the showing of a nine-minute video about Benton's contentious artwork, and students are given cards on which to write their personal reactions to the mural. If students still feel that the climate is hostile, they should first discuss the matter with a faculty member, and, if that is still not adequate, they should contact the IU Bloomington Racial Incidents Team in their quest for closure. Ah, there, I've uttered it, 'that ghastly word *closure*' (Gore Vidal). The good thing is that (for now) the mural has not been removed or covered up and that Benton's work has been drawn to the attention of a larger audience, its 'Michelangelesque distortions' (I quote from Nan Brewer's essay) and all; the bad news is that IU exhibited an equivocalness at odds with both its scholarly mission and its exemplary history of supporting freedom of thought and expression—Indiana University, after all, was home to Alfred Kinsey whose pioneering studies of human sexuality are still too much for some Hoosier natives to stomach.

I grew up in a country where dark deeds have been perpetrated for centuries by one group or another; deeds that have often been recorded in paintings, sculptures, literature, music and verse. The history of Ireland includes representations that, inevitably, conjure up searing memories for one side or the other. Mention the names of Cromwell or King Billy to an Irish Catholic and wait for the sulfurous reaction. For centuries, limited civil rights were granted to the minority population of Northern Ireland, but no one has ever suggested that these historic injustices can be undone, or atoned for, by expunging or sugarcoating elements of the country's Protestant artistic and cultural heritage. Oliver ('To Hell or Connaught') Cromwell and William of Orange are perduring elements of the country's complex and at times bloody history. Ireland has its Benton murals, as a sightseeing tour of post-Troubles Belfast will make abundantly clear, but we can, just about, live with them. W.H. Auden—whose visit to IU and the bowels of the Lilly Library is the stuff of a wonderful anecdote told by Donald Gray, but not for thunder-stealing retelling here—wrote in his essay *The Public v. the Late Mr William Butler Yeats* that 'art is a product of history, not a cause.' History, however painful, needs to be taught, not sanitized or separated from its 'products.' And where better to do that than at a research university?

Historical airbrushing—what the Romans termed *damnatio memoriae*—is an extraordinarily dangerous path to go down: who draws the line, and where? Not, I trust, the Black Student Union—or any other student union, for that matter. Is art without veracity set to join coffee without caffeine, beer without alcohol, and cigarettes without nicotine in our neutered age? If the Benton murals are to be secreted away to avoid causing offense to a hypersensitive minority, should the curtain also come down on Picasso's *Guernica*? Should *Mein Kampf* be removed from the shelves? Should Wagner's music not be performed in Israel? It's a short and slippery slope from banning Benton in Bloomington to blasting the Buddhas of Bamiyan. Diversity engineering has no place in matters art-historical. In truth, it has no place in a university.

Monet Makes the World Go Round

I like paintings. In fact, I often like them so much that I buy them. This is good news for starving artists, not such good news for my starving children. I can't help it. Like my father and grandfather I am a compulsive collector.

Bloomington is awash with weekend daubers—and I'm not referring to the urban artists, whose graffiti embellish the inter-state rolling stock that rumbles through, and occasional pauses in, the town's little known sidings—but few of these daubers are blessed with genuine talent. I have yet to leave the John Waldron Arts Center feeling especially uplifted, but, then, abstract quilts and *papier-mâché* sculptures have never been my thing. You might be luckier, though, at one of the regular student shows organized by the Henry Radford Hope School of Fine Arts; SoFA is among the oldest (though not among the very best) university art departments in the United States, and was founded in 1895.

At least painting is a civilized past-time, one that keeps Bloomingtonians out of harm's way while keeping Pygmalion's in business. A few miles due west in scenic Nashville you'll encounter a slightly more expert breed of dauber. This long-established artists' colony continues to attract painterly types, though few, even on a good day, seem to achieve the heights. If you think I'm being gratuitously rude, just take a quick trip to the Brown County Art Gallery in downtown Nashville and follow that up with a tour of local galleries and studios. There ain't no budding Bacons or Basquiats in Brown County. Nor in Monroe County, for that matter, though some may conceivably be taken with the multitalented Mr. Mellencamp's expressive portraiture (like mother, like son). If Hoosiers have a favorite international artist, it must surely be Fernando Botero, whose pneumatic figures are so reassuringly familiar.

T.C. Steele, the Daddy of all Hoosier Daubers, was no great shakes, truth be told; a regional star, a local *plein air* patriarch, at best. Many of the paintings hanging in his studio adjacent to the 'House of the Singing Winds,' where he captured, patiently and persistently, the light and leaves of southern Indiana, have a flatness and heaviness of hand about them. The eye travels quickly by. A couple, though, remind me somewhat of the Irish artist, Nathaniel Hone, and after a pint or two of strong cider I might even invoke, admittedly in foolhardy fashion, the name of Corot. But you don't need to traipse to Nashville to take the measure of Steele; several of his landscapes are to be found in the vicinity of the Tudor Room in the Indiana Memorial Union: sad to say, I have yet to see anyone pause to look at them, even though they are undeniably easy on the eye. My favorite Steele canvas, on display in the IU Art Museum, may just be the muscularly realistic 'Boatman'— painted when the artist was a student at the Royal Academy of Fine Arts in Munich in 1884: it's as far removed from a chocolate box cover as could be.

The Art Museum's collection of paintings—never mind its holdings of ancient and African art—is quite an eye-opener, ranging all the way from *quattrocento* delights to conceptual teasers. Here you'll find Balthus, Braque, Dubuffet, Lichtenstein, Monet, Picasso, Pollock and Rouault a mere alcove away from a poor man's Fra Angelico. This isn't the Fogg, but one can easily become misty eyed. It's free and all too often, from a curatorial perspective, deserted. The Museum's 35,000 or so holdings would put many a metropolitan collection to shame. And then there's its director, Heidi Gealt, a recognized authority on Domenico Tiepolo (son of *über*-Dauber, Giambattista Tiepolo), co-author of *Domenico Tiepolo: A New Testament* and guest curator, at the Frick, of the parallel exhibition. It's all too good to be true, not that the bulk of the student population seems to know or care: for them Art is the guy who sang with Paul Simon in Central Park.

If you're a compulsive purchaser of paintings, Bloomington is a good place to be. Temptation rarely gets its act together. For that we have to thank the local talent, whose idea of art, annually and keenly exhibited at the 4th Street Festival of Arts and Crafts and the charming Arts Fair on the Square, would not be out of place in the more desperate parts of Canyon Road, Santa Fe. If, however, you're a lazy collector and want no more than a marquee name or two to hang in the dining room to impress the impressionable ('wall power'), then a trip to the Middle Way Benefit Auction is probably your best bet. Here you'll typically find a signed lithograph by Chagall, Braque or Picasso, donated anonymously and bid for ostentatiously. Of course, eBay is awash in hand-signed, limited edition prints by the likes of Braque and Dalí, but *caveat emptor* I say to those who would venture into this market. Still, if you enjoy the idea of a live, public sale whipped along by a bow-legged auctioneer who seems to think he is selling longhorns rather than lithographs, then why not? The pain of parting with your hard-earned dollars will be eased by the complimentary snacks, cash bar and gentle sounds provided by the IU Early Music Institute, not to mention the prospect of pointing insouciantly to your proto-Picasso during next Saturday's soirée.

But occasionally a pearl can be spotted among the local swine. For fifteen years I have been buying works by Tamar Kander, who came to Middle America from South Africa by way of Israel, London and New York. She forsook That Road in Bloomington—I have a dry point etching of that very road, her actual postal address—for Brown County, but no sin is unforgivable.

Typically she produces what I'd term abstract landscapes, of here and elsewhere; layered gobs and knobs of goo and gesso, cement and pigment, trowelled and scratched into large canvases—intimations of Tàpies (whom I also discovered for the first time in the Ulster Museum). She would take issue with such a trite characterization of her work: 'closely linked to jazz, music in its many forms, and really to the space between things, not the things themselves,' would be her retort. But, while I can tell a Homer from a Hopper, I'm no art critic; Thom Rea is, and has written perceptively about Kander in the *Herald-Times*: '…an abstract painter who uses the most rugged materials to create the most delicate, poetic effects.' He has considerably more to say. Now, I wouldn't bet the shop that the gracious Tamar will ever be a saleroom name, or feature in *ARTnews*, but she does show with galleries in Bloomington, Indianapolis, Louisville, Chicago, Atlanta and Santa Fe, so clearly others also see the something that I see.

For some artists, like Kander, Bloomington and its hinterland can be their implausible muse. Once more, the cynics may have to eat their words, or, like Van Gough, their oil paints. Scratch the surface of the canvas of life in Bloomington, and you may just be surprised by what lies beneath.

Happy What?

Christmas is celebrated across the globe by Christians and non-Christians alike. The religious origins and significance of the festival matter deeply to some; not a jot to others. But a fine time can be had by one and all. For good or ill, Christmas has been secularized and commercialized. That trend is irreversible. Christmas has long since transcended its denominational roots; Christianity no longer owns Christmas.

It is a time when most of us wind down and enjoy the comforting if clichéd paraphernalia of the bleakest season; scented fir trees, pine-encrusted wreaths, ruddy Santas, Yule logs, jingling bells, twinkling lights and Bing Crosby. Bloomington and Christmas go together like Laurel and Hardy; the place sparkles and when dusted with snow can look like a giant Hallmark card come to life. Christmas brings much of the Western world to a grinding halt, and brings many of us together in a way that no other religious holiday or folk festival can. One can but imagine what it means to the inhabitants of Santa Claus, a town in Spencer County, Indiana.

Christmas is a unique, if schizophrenic, event in our culture. For more than half a century I have routinely wished people 'Merry Christmas.' It was what one did because it was Christmas, a holiday that was universally acknowledged and celebrated by almost all. Other faiths have their holy days and religious traditions, but neither Hanukkah nor Ramadan can be compared with Christmas. And as for Kwanza!

This year the Catholic League placed an ad attacking 'cultural fascists' in the *New York Times*. It began: 'The United States is 85 percent Christian, which means we are more Christian than India is Hindu and Israel is Jewish. Moreover, 96 percent of Americans celebrate Christmas.' You don't have to believe in Christ or be a child of Christendom to understand the cross-cultural significance and unifying power of Christmas. Heathens (such as myself) can enjoy the sight and smell of a Christmas tree as much as true believers. And the residents of Richmond, Virginia, certainly enjoy twinkling lights; one of the houses featured on the city's 'Tacky Lights Tours' boasted 170,000 bulbs. But I am drifting off-piste.

Regrettably, Christmas has become, in the jargon of academics, problematized. Most of my colleagues pussyfoot around the word, rarely daring to wish anyone 'Merry Christmas.' Instead, we are fobbed off with 'Happy Holidays,' which is fine if one is heading off for a summer vacation in Tuscany, but plain silly in the case of Christmas. We all know it's Christmas, we all trim Christmas trees, we all buy Christmas presents, we all send Christmas cards, we all over-indulge on Christmas Day…but we can't bring ourselves to conjoin 'Merry' and 'Christmas' in the logical, seasonal salutation. Such are the cultural politics of Xmas.

The rot set in locally some years ago when a high-minded law professor on the Indianapolis campus (and local ACLU board member), Florence Wagman Roisman, objected to the presence of a Christmas tree in the Law School atrium, some non-Christian students having claimed that they felt 'excluded.' A pusillanimous dean, since departed, duly had it removed—a sorry harbinger of this year's dismantling of the Christmas tree at Seattle-Tacoma International Airport, a ludicrous act that was reversed as a result of justifiable public outrage. For the record, a Christmas tree is not a religious symbol in the way that either a nativity scene or menorah is. But the Law School is not the only culprit at IU; other units have followed suit. Send them all a DVD of *The Grinch Who Stole Christmas*, I say.

This year's (unsigned) Christmas card from President Herbert and his wife (whom I've never met) referred in anodyne fashion to 'the holiday season.' However, my mood brightened when I saw that the IU Auditorium was presenting 'Chimes of Christmas' rather than 'Chimes of Holidays' which will include classic carols such as 'We Wish You a Merry Christmas;' no titular blue-lining here. The IU Libraries staff newsletter went one better with a no-holds-barred 'Merry Christmas' on its seasonal issue. All is not yet lost.

While the Gownies fret endlessly about political correctness and multiculturalism, the Townies seem on the whole to prefer the traditional greeting, at least according to a story ('Merry Christmas or Generic Greeting?') in the *Herald-Times*. And corporate America, too, may be coming to its senses: a spokeswoman for Wal-Mart stated that 'Christmas is back at Wal-Mart. If you walk into a Wal-Mart store this year, you will see and hear the words Merry Christmas.' Apparently, this *volte-face*, when announced at the company's seasonal planning conference, was greeted with 'thunderous applause' by 7,000 Wal-Mart managers. If only we Gownies had as much common sense as the good burghers of Bloomington, not to mention the vast majority of the American populace.

Wheels up!

You'll die if you live here. Spiritually, I mean. Bloomington, for all its subtle appeal, cannot provide the full complement of nutrients the soul craves. What city can? Every so often we sessile radicals have to break away from our limestone base, say goodbye to the *vita contemplativa*, and re-engage with the real world, where overcrowding, rudeness and stress are energy-sapping facts of daily life. Coming up for air, as it were, can remind us just how lucky we are to be where we are, especially if Mogadishu or Lagos happens to be our first port of call.

Gownies are by calling peripatetic beasts. Our conference caravans wisely stop off at the choicest locations, just long enough for us to present a paper, refresh our social networks and rate the local cuisine. Foreign travel is one of the principal (as yet untaxed—and long may it be so) perquisites of academic life, and brings with it limitless opportunities for fun, frolics and fame. David Lodge and Malcolm Bradbury have probably said all that needs to be said on that subject. My lips, I assure you, are forever sealed. As for the Townies, their horizons are rather more limited. For them, Cincinnati is a destination; for us it's a *point de départ.*

It took me a decade to discover that one could fly direct from Cincinnati to half a dozen European capitals, including London and Paris; no more missed connections and lost luggage at hellish O'Hare and chaotic JFK. The drive to Cincinnati (two hours with a tailwind; two and a half with the cops sitting on your tail) takes you over the gently rolling hills of south central Indiana, past Barn Yard Friends (not, as you might think, the headquarters of a bestiality website but home to a miscellany of animals including, most incongruously for this latitude, a camel), through the kitsch charms of Nashville—a cluster of wooden clapboard houses and white picket fences that somehow isn't quite the sum of its picture postcard parts—and past tiny Gnaw Bone, home to the self-proclaimed, world-famous Gnaw Bone Tenderloin.

The name, allegedly, derives from a French settlement, Narbonne, which English settlers translated literally as Gnaw Bone. It's a place in name only, as far as I can tell; half a dozen shacks, acres of flea markets brimming with rusted plowshares and not a steakhouse in sight. Gnaw Bone, this grotesquely improbable locus of culinary sophistication, is a far cry from the restored splendor of French Lick with its famous sulphur water: 'When nature won't work, Pluto will.' But French Lick and West Baden Springs are for another day, another drive.

From Gnaw Bone it's only a 15-minute spurt to the holy of architectural holies, Columbus. Tarry a while here and you'll discover buildings designed by a number of modern 'starchitects' such as Robert Venturi, I.M. Pei (his use of poured concrete rather than limestone on the Bloomington campus is still a gnawable bone of contention for some) and, most notably, Eero Saarinen, whose other credits include the emblematic Gateway Arch in St. Louis. For all its architectural significance, I find self-congratulatory Columbus (Athens of the Prairie) eerily bland as an urban space. It has no life, no convincing center. Invariably, I come away with a vague feeling of melancholy.

But onwards to Cincinnati, where the country road to Greensburg slices through cornfields, tall and wide enough to hide an army of Maasai warriors. Tennyson comes to mind: 'On either side the river lie / Long fields of barley and of rye, / That clothe the wold and meet the sky; /...' Here you get a real sense of the Midwest, of the panoramas photographed lovingly by Art Sinsabaugh (the IU Art Museum has a splendid collection of his work—more than 3,000 items): big skies and yawning vistas studded with red-stained barns and dildo-like grain silos. This is stolid, middle America, a world made up of decent folks, hard work and uncomplicated protestant values. It deserves respect, not bicoastal sneers. The return journey on an early winter evening can be spell-binding, the leafless trees and farmsteads silhouetted against a Joseph's coat of burnt orange, purple, pink, carmine and midnight blue.

Cincinnati airport is commendably efficient and now boasts a Wolfgang Puck for flying foodies. Look out for the homoerotic, neo-Soviet Realistic artwork at international check-in (shades of Benton's *Coal, Gas, Oil, Brick*—Industrial Panel 9) and don't on any account miss the Freedom Shrine before passing though the heavy-handed security. The mere sight of this mawkish display always makes me wonder what on earth I'm doing in this part of the world. Delta may be teetering interminably on the edge of bankruptcy, but to the ailing airline's credit its planes consistently take off and land on time and for reasons I cannot quite fathom the cabin crews take evident, albeit sometimes rather self-conscious, pleasure in serving their transatlantic customers, even those of us in coach class. It's almost too good to be true: Europe within the arc of the accessible.

Seven and a half hours after 'Wheels up!', Bloomington, this mildly eccentric but *gemütlich* bastion of *belles lettres*, music and the performing arts tucked away in the heartland, is replaced by the cultural Mother Lode and instantly forgotten. The Regency splendor of Brighton, all pilasters and capitals, fanlights and architraves, reigns supreme. But it's not long before we start hankering after peace and quiet and yearning against our better judgment for the block chords of daily life in B-town: the friendly and not so friendly fauna, the baleful lowing of freight trains, the civic pride and PC silliness, our potty fixation with gender-neutral bathrooms, the 'In God We Trust' license plates (brainchild, for want of a better word, of state representative Woody Burton, brother of U.S. congressman Dan Burton, once referred to by the *Indianapolis Star* as 'the biggest skirt-chaser in the Indiana legislature'), the amateur passions, and the faculty foibles that make Bloomington's particular blend of Town and Gown so damnably difficult to resist.

Soon the hankering is more akin to phantom limb pain. So back we go, whizzing past Pease Pottage, Lower Beeding and the high jumps of Hickstead, to the Delta check-in desk at bustling Gatwick, thence, in the time it takes to cull the perpetual backlog of well-traveled *New Yorkers* and develop deep vein thrombosis, to the zany world of Delta Zeta, Alpha Delta and all rest of the garbled Greek alphabet. And then, just as surely as night follows day, we start pining all over again for Albion and her fading, though still irresistible, charms.

About The Author

Blaise Cronin was born and raised in Ireland. Trinity College Dublin and the Queen's University of Belfast graciously granted him the degrees necessary to avoid working for a living. He came to Middle America via London (England) and Glasgow (Scotland). In one sense, he has never looked back; in another, he has never stopped looking back.

Printed in the United Kingdom
by Lightning Source UK Ltd.
124592UK00003BC/309/A